MW00636700

SHE DID

ordinary women, extraordinary faith

EMILY CUSHING & BEKKI HOOD

DESERET
BOOK

TO MY MOM AND THREE SISTERS—
THE FIRST OF MANY WOMEN
WHO HAVE INFLUENCED MY LIFE
—EC

TO MY FAMILY—
MOM, DAD, KRISTIN, KYLIE, & BRIGHAM
—BH

© 2023 Emily Cushing and Bekki Hood

All rights reserved. No part of this book may be reproduced in any form or by any means without permission in writing from the publisher, Deseret Book Company, at permissions@deseretbook.com. This work is not an official publication of The Church of Jesus Christ of Latter-day Saints. The views expressed herein are the responsibility of the authors and do not necessarily represent the position of the Church or of Deseret Book Company.

DESERET BOOK is a registered trademark of Deseret Book Company.

Visit us at deseretbook.com

Library of Congress Cataloging-in-Publication Data
CIP on file
ISBN 978-1-63993-132-3

Printed in China
RR Donnelley, Dongguan, China

10 9 8 7 6 5 4 3 2 1

Contents

CONTENTS

CONTENTS

Introduction

"Let us not just endure this current season. Let us embrace the future with faith." **PRESIDENT RUSSELL M. NELSON**

The idea to write a book about the lives of extraordinary Latter-day Saint women came to me years ago. I listened to a general conference talk about Aurelia Spencer, the founder of the Primary, and another about Irene Corbett, a Latter day Saint nurse who sailed on the *Titanic*.[1] These two women amazed me. They displayed faith and courage in the face of extreme difficulties. I was so inspired that I wanted to share their stories. So what did I do?

Nothing.

My "real life" as a wife and a mother to five busy children was a little too "real" at the time, so my book idea continued to be just that, an idea. It wasn't until I opened a book about famous women who had made a difference in the world that I was reminded of Aurelia and Irene. The women in the book had dedicated their time to improving the lives of others, but so had Aurelia, Irene, and so many other Latter-day Saint women. Primary had been an important part of my childhood, yet before listening to the talk about Aurelia, I had no idea it had been founded by a woman who had crossed the plains as a parentless teenager with her younger siblings in tow. And I had always been intrigued by the details of the sinking of the *Titanic*, but until I learned about Irene, I didn't know that onboard there had been a courageous Latter-day Saint woman who had studied medicine to help protect mothers and infants during child-birth. Aurelia and Irene may not have been famous by the world's standards, but they too had made a difference—within their homes, communities, and the Church. In ways I hadn't realized, they had made a difference in my home as well. A fire sparked within me, and I knew it was time to bring their stories to light.

I enlisted a brilliant coauthor, Bekki Hood, and we began search-ing for more Latter-day Saint women to include in the book—women who, despite heartache, tragedy, or discouragement, followed the scriptures' counsel to "go and do" (see 1 Nephi 3:7). The "goings and doings" of these women are the driving force behind this book. Indifference, apathy, and idleness may thrive in the world, but this book celebrates the untold stories of Latter-day Saint women who went and did. They dreamed, they influenced, they helped, they led, they empowered, they inspired, they persevered, but most of all, they embraced the future with faith no matter their circumstances.

The lives of valiant Latter-day Saint women stretch across time and the globe. Providing a glimpse of their enduring and worldwide influence, this book features women of varying races, ethnicities, cul-tures, and places. The women range from missionaries to mothers and athletes to authors, and their lives span nearly a century and a half, from pioneer days to the present.

These are stories of women who maintained trust in the Lord and believed in doing what's right, regardless of circumstance or conse-quence. One defended her faith at gunpoint when soldiers stormed a mission home, while another humbly shared her testimony until the age of 109.

These are stories of women who set good examples, ministered to others, and brought many to Christ by sharing the gospel. One helped to build a bridge between cultures during a divisive period in the United States, while another was the first missionary in her homeland of India.

These are stories of women who used their abilities, resources, and wits to provide for themselves and their families. One relocated herself and her four surviving children after her husband and son were murdered, while another knelt in prayer asking Heavenly Father to watch over her son who had chosen a dangerous path.

These are stories of women who offered suggestions, solved problems, and fearlessly used their voices for change. One founded a nonprofit organization to bring hope to those suffering from Hansen's disease, while another spoke on a national platform to advance women's rights.

These remarkable stories are just a sampling of the millions of Latter-day Saint women and girls worldwide who live faithfully. These women draw on their courage and testimonies of the Savior to face and triumph over loss, illness, poverty, divorce, discrimination, and family conflict. And then the world is changed. Even if it's only the world of one or two.

Most of the women in this book didn't realize at the time that their actions would have such a significant impact on others. Likewise, there are countless Latter-day Saint women whose seemingly ordinary actions—ministering to others, receiving personal revelation, magnifying callings, building up families, and pursuing light and knowledge—have an extraordinary influence on those around them.

While spending countless hours researching each featured woman's life, Bekki and I felt inspired to become better daughters, neighbors, ministering sisters, and disciples of Christ. Our circumstances are quite different—Bekki is a single woman juggling two careers, and I'm busy raising a family and working part-time. But we both found stories that spoke to us in personal and meaningful ways. We both felt the call to "go and do." We hope the same will be true for all readers of this book. The actions of a few might seem inconsequential, but in following the guidance of the Lord and the promptings of the Spirit, when "she did" is combined with "I did," "they did," and "we did," we invoke a spiritual power that makes a difference and changes the world in extraordinary ways.

—emily and bekki

Amanda
Barnes Smith

1809–1886

Survivor of Hawn's Mill Massacre

"Fear thou not; for I am with thee: be not dismayed; for I am thy God: I will strengthen thee; yea, I will help thee; yea, I will uphold thee with the right hand of my righteousness." ISAIAH 41:10

A DARK DAY

Amanda and her family weren't supposed to be at Hawn's Mill when a mob of over two hundred men attacked the small settlement. She and her husband, Warren, had been traveling with their five young children from Kirtland, Ohio, to join the Saints in Far West, Missouri, a distance of over eight hundred miles. After six difficult months of travel, they stopped to camp for a few days at Hawn's Mill, a Latter-day Saint settlement consisting of about seventy-five families. Their timing couldn't have been worse, for they would soon find themselves in the middle of one of the darkest days in Church history.[1]

For several years, tension and confrontations between Latter-day Saints and Missourians had been growing. Two days before Amanda and her family arrived at Hawn's Mill, Governor Lilburn Boggs signed an "extermination order," giving permission for Latter-day Saints to be removed from Missouri by any means necessary. When the Prophet Joseph Smith heard about the order, he counseled the Saints in outlying settlements to gather to Far West.[2] But his message was never delivered to the families at Hawn's Mill.[3]

In the late afternoon of October 30, 1838, an armed mob of about 240 men with painted faces rode into the camp at Hawn's Mill. Without warning, they opened fire on the men, women, and children in the camp. Many of the men ran for the blacksmith's shop, taking the little boys with them. They yelled, "We surrender!" But the mob ignored their pleas and continued shooting. Seeing the mob's determination to exterminate the Latter-day Saints, the men in the blacksmith shop shouted to their wives to take the children and run for their lives. As bullets flew thickly around them, Amanda and her two daughters fled into the nearby woods to hide.

With its widely spaced log walls, the blacksmith's shop became a deathtrap. The attackers surrounded the shop and fired over 1,600 bullets at the vulnerable structure, killing almost everyone inside and anyone who came out to surrender. The mob ransacked all of the tents and cabins, stealing their victims' money, belongings, and horses. As the mob rode away, they howled with laughter. Seventeen Latter-day Saints were murdered, including Amanda's husband, Warren, and their ten-year-old son, Sardius.

A MIRACLE

After the attack, Amanda's eleven-year-old son, Willard, entered the blacksmith shop. There he found a survivor: his six-year-old brother, Alma, whose hip had been blown away. Willard gently picked him up and carried him outside. When Amanda emerged from the woods and saw Willard carrying a bloodied Alma, she screamed, "They have killed my little Alma!" Willard explained that he was alive but that his father and Sardius had been killed. Having seen the carnage in the blacksmith shop, Willard begged his mother not to go inside, but to help him with Alma.

Amanda and Willard took Alma to their looted tent and made him a bed of straw and clothing. Amanda gathered the rest of her children around her and prayed to Heavenly Father, begging for inspiration and guidance on how to save her little boy. She received revelation to take ashes from the fireplace and make a lye solution, which she used to clean mangled flesh and bone from the gaping wound. She was then prompted to use the roots from an elm tree to make a soothing poultice.[4]

Despite Amanda's constant fear that the mob would attack again, Alma couldn't be moved and had to lie belly down—in the same position—for five weeks. Because of this, she and her four children had to stay near Hawn's Mill. Whenever men from the mob returned, she did everything she could to protect her family, yelling out threats to anyone who approached.[5] One day she was so distraught she crawled into a cornfield to pray. She heard a voice—not a silent, strong impression, but a distinct *voice*—repeating the final verse of the hymn "How Firm a Foundation." It gave her strength and the confirmation that her family would be protected and God would heal her son. From that point on, her fear disappeared, and Alma miraculously made a full recovery.

In the aftermath of the Hawn's Mill Massacre, Amanda and other widowed Latter-day Saint women met together for daily prayer meetings. They continued doing this until they were restricted by local antagonists.

FAITH-FILLED FEARLESSNESS

Widowed and penniless, Amanda had to decide what to do next. Hardship and discomfort weren't new to her. She had been disowned by her parents when she joined the Church, and she and Warren had lost most of their land and possessions when the Kirtland Bank had failed. Through disappointment and despair, Amanda had always been resilient; she persevered and depended on her Heavenly Father's guidance. This time was no different. When Alma was strong enough to be moved, she knew it was time to leave the state of Missouri.

But first, she needed to get her horses back.

She traveled ten miles to the home of Captain Comstock, who was the leader of the mob, and fearlessly demanded the horse he had stolen during the massacre. While Comstock's wife swore at him that he'd been a fool for not killing the women and children as well as the men, he told Amanda she could have her horse for five dollars. Because the Lord had promised Amanda in the cornfield that her family would be protected, she didn't fear Comstock. She walked into his yard, tied her apron around her horse's neck, and led it away without permission or resistance. Learning that her other horse was being kept at a mill, she went there next. When she arrived, Comstock was waiting. Because of Amanda's determination and the remorse he felt over murdering the Saints, he not only gave back her other horse but also gave her beef, a can of honey, and fifty pounds of flour.[6] Amanda took these provisions and led her four small children hundreds of miles to Illinois to start a new life once again.[7]

> Amanda was described as "an indefatigable laborer . . . among the poor and sick ministering to both their spiritual and temporal needs."

EMBRACING THE FUTURE WITH FAITH

Once Amanda and her family settled in Illinois, she became a schoolteacher to support her family. She was also a member of the first Relief Society. She married another Warren Smith (not related to her first husband), and they had three children. He already had five children, which made her the mother of thirteen. Although she had dared to love and marry again, she had to leave Warren because he was unfaithful and abusive. Though setting out on her own again, especially at a time when women usually depended on their husbands for financial security, was a difficult decision, Amanda put herself and her children first and left Warren shortly after they moved to Utah in 1850. In Salt Lake City, Amanda helped organize the Sunday School and Relief Society.

Even when tragedy and hardship were thrust in Amanda's path, she continued to press forward in faith. She made a difference by honoring her religious and civic duties—she raised funds for people in need, defended the Church, and advocated for women's suffrage. But most of all, she constantly bore a strong testimony and recognized God's hand in her life. Whenever a doctor heard about her son Alma's ordeal and asked Amanda how she had performed the surgery that saved him, Amanda replied that it was Jesus Christ who had healed him.[8] Alma was able to live a full life and walk without difficulty. He went on to marry, have nine children, and serve four missions.[9]

Amanda's son Alma Smith

Before her death in 1886, Amanda described her life as a "checkered scene of joy and trouble. I have drank the dregs of the cup of sorrow and affliction, as well as partaken of the blessings of an all-wise merciful God." Through it all, Amanda held fast to the lyrics that had been spoken to her that day in the cornfield: "The soul that on Jesus hath leaned for repose, I will not, I cannot desert to his foes; That soul, though all hell should endeavor to shake, I'll never, no never, . . . no never forsake!"

Mary Dunster Chittenden

1818–1886

Believer Who Left a Legacy of Faith

"In all thy ways acknowledge him, and he shall direct thy paths." **PROVERBS 3:6**

MARY'S DREAMS

Shortly after the death of her second baby boy in 1853, Mary dreamed she met two men carrying satchels. One of them held out a little book to her. In her dream, she felt that the book was important, and even though she couldn't read, she took it, hoping her children would read it to her. A few months after her dream, her husband traveled from Camden, Australia, where they lived, to Sydney, where his friend introduced him to two missionaries from The Church of Jesus Christ of Latter-day Saints.[1] William heard their message of the restored gospel and instantly believed it was true.[2]

At the time, missionaries relied on the generosity of others to provide them with food and shelter, so when John invited the missionaries to travel home with him, they readily agreed. When they arrived at the Chittenden home, Mary recognized the missionaries' Book of Mormon as the important book she had dreamed about and knew it was a fulfillment of her vision.[3] Despite negative rumors circulating in Australia about the Latter-day Saints, Mary knew the

Mary was described as "a medium-sized, well-built woman, with kind gray eyes and a pleasant but firm mouth. Her step was quick and her manner filled of warm-hearted simplicity."

gospel was true. She and her husband, William, were baptized in 1854.

When the Chittendens joined the Church, they became outcasts among their neighbors and friends. So when elders from the United States described how Zion was being built up in the Salt Lake Valley, with tree-lined streets at the base of beautiful mountains, Mary desperately wanted to pack up her family and move to Utah. William, however, was a quiet, determined man, and even though their large farm was prospering, he knew they wouldn't be able to afford the travel expenses for himself, Mary, and their eight children.[4]

MONEY TO MOVE

Undeterred, Mary looked for ways to earn extra money. She was thrifty and had a good eye for business. When the father of a motherless seven-year-old boy heard Mary was the disciplinarian to her obedient children and kept an extremely clean home, he offered to pay Mary to let the boy live with her family. Unaware of the boy's mischievous nature or the havoc he'd wreak, Mary agreed. One Sunday the boy thought he'd have some fun. He found a box of matches and snuck down to the pig pens where nobody would see

him. He lit a tiny fire, which burned quietly at first, but then the wind caught hold of the flame and carried it onto the roof of a pig pen. By the time the boy ran for help, the entire yard was in flames. Despite the Chittendens' best efforts to stop the fire, it sputtered, crackled, and leapt until it had engulfed animals, barns,

Mary with her husband, William

the granary, and even part of their home. Although neighbors saw the fire on their way to their own churches, nobody stopped to help. The Chittendens lost almost everything.

That night Mary sat outside with her two-week-old baby wailing in her arms. Household goods were broken and scattered around her. Her comfortable home was blackened, and like the smoke drifting up from the walls of her home, her bright hopes and plans to immigrate to the United States disappeared into the night. How was she ever going to fulfill her dream of immigrating now?[5]

Just as a dream had led Mary to the gospel, yet another dream helped her and her family after the devastating fire, which had left them nearly destitute. In this vision, her family was prompted to sell their few belongings and move to a frontier town called Goulburn in the southwest region of Australia. Her family heeded the prompting and moved to Goulburn, where Mary used her skills as a healer to earn money. Although Mary had never received formal nursing training, she was often sent for when someone was having a baby or required medical assistance. Mary was able to once again start saving funds to move to Utah.

EMBRACING THE FUTURE WITH FAITH

On April 7, 1877, at the age of fifty-eight, Mary finally accomplished her goal when she boarded a ship for America with her husband, her three youngest children, and a granddaughter. Their additional daughters—all nine of them—were married and stayed in Australia with their families.[6]

When the Chittendens settled in Provo, Utah, they

Although Mary saved money to travel to Utah, the Chittendens' resources were used, foremost, for their children's schooling. Mary and William had not received a formal education, and they were adamant that their children have this great blessing in their lives.

had less than ten dollars to their names. William had become extremely ill with a kidney disease, so Mary and her daughters went to work. Mary took in laundry, which she washed in a large tub, and her daughters labored in a factory. Less than a year after they moved to Utah, William lay dying. He called their thirteen-year-old son, Hyrum, to his bedside.[7] William asked Hyrum to promise he'd take Mary to the temple one day. At the time, there was only one temple, and it was located in St. George, Utah, and the Chittendens didn't have the money to make the 250-mile trip.[8] Hyrum promised that he would.

A couple years after William passed away, Mary had yet another dream. The same personage who had come to her in a previous vision appeared and told her it was time for her to go to the temple and perform the saving ordinances for herself and her husband. The personage promised that if she did, she'd have a home soon afterwards. By this time Hyrum was a tall, quiet-mannered sixteen-year-old. He worked tirelessly carrying large chains on surveying expeditions. One night he gave Mary a hundred dollars and told her he wanted to take her to the temple so he could fulfill the promise he'd made to his father. She revealed her vision to him, and that very night Hyrum went to the bishop and received permission to do his father's temple work.

> "Obey the whisperings of God, trusting to Him for the result!"
>
> MARY CHITTENDEN

A year after their trip to the temple, Mary and Hyrum had saved enough money to bargain for a lot in Provo, where they built a small home with two little rooms.[9] Mary lived there comfortably until she passed away on July 2, 1886, at the age of sixty-seven.[10]

Some of Mary's other children eventually immigrated to the United States, but those who stayed in Australia continued to teach the gospel to their children and share it with their neighbors. Mary's daughter Jane held sacrament meetings in her home, and the home of Mary's other daughter, Alice, doubled as the mission headquarters. Both Jane and Alice provided beds, meals, and laundry services for the missionaries and kept them busy with investigators referred to them by friends and members of their extended family. By the year 1900, nearly a quarter of the Sydney Branch were descendants of the Chittendens. Throughout Australia, as well as in many parts of the

Australia's first Latter-day Saint meetinghouse, built in 1904 and located in Woolloongabba, near Brisbane

United States and Canada, Mary left a legacy of strong faith that helped spread the gospel and strengthen the Church.[11]

Aurelia
Spencer Rogers

1834–1922

Founder of the Primary Organization

"Wherefore, be not weary in well-doing, for ye are laying the foundation of a great work. And out of small things proceedeth that which is great." **DOCTRINE AND COVENANTS 64:33**

A CHILD OF ADVERSITY AND RESPONSIBILITY

Aurelia and Ellen feverishly opened the latest letter from their father, Orson Spencer, who was serving a mission in Great Britain. In his letter, he wrote with love and affection, "My oldest daughters; on you is rolled a great responsibility, seemingly beyond your years. Be womanly, kind, and patient, act the part of mother to the younger children."[1] Aurelia was not your average twelve-year-old. Since her mother had died and her father had left for his mission, Aurelia and her fourteen-year-old sister, Ellen, were given charge of their four younger siblings. Though children themselves, Aurelia and Ellen were the primary caregivers for the parentless family.

The Spencer children lived in an unfinished single-room log cabin in Winter Quarters, Nebraska. Although they lived close to kind neighbors who offered food, companionship, and clothing, their life in the Latter-day Saint settlement was trying. The Saints suffered through brutal winters with freezing temperatures, heavy snowfall, and fierce winds that

As a child Aurelia was a sleepwalker who would wander to a bench behind the stove, where she sat until her parents quietly led her back to bed.

chilled them to the bone. Measles and other diseases swept through the settlement. Aurelia and her siblings nursed one another through illnesses, while death raged relentlessly among other families. Nearly all of the Spencers' livestock had died, and the money that their father sent them was often lost or stolen in transit. Amid illness and poverty, Aurelia endeavored to create a home for her siblings—a place where they felt safe, a place where they felt loved, and a place where the Spirit could reside.[2]

That a group of children could endure such challenges seems inexplicable, but Aurelia's family had built a spiritual foundation that helped them brave the fiercest of storms. When Aurelia was six years old, her parents chose to join The Church of Jesus Christ of Latter-day Saints, a decision that brought on scorn from their neighbors and forced them to leave a comfortable lifestyle. The Spencers joined the Saints in Nauvoo, Illinois, where they would eventually grieve the martyrdom of their beloved prophet, Joseph Smith. The family's foundation was forged in sacrifice, and more was soon asked of them.[3]

While the children lived in Winter Quarters, the prophet Brigham Young asked their permission to keep their father in England. He also invited them to travel west in his wagon company. Although they missed their father terribly and hundreds of miles stood between them and Salt Lake City, Aurelia and her siblings agreed to the prophet's request, sacrificing all that they had once more to build the kingdom of God.[4]

In the spring of 1848, Aurelia and Ellen packed their family's meager belongings and led their younger siblings through harsh conditions and rough terrain. For five months, the little family journeyed a thousand miles on foot until they arrived in the Salt Lake Valley. They made their home in an old fort, and Aurelia tried to provide for the family by selling bracelets and necklaces made from hair. One year after they arrived in Utah, Orson Spencer returned home from his mission and joyfully reunited with his family after being separated from them for three long years.[5]

Aurelia described herself as being "as happy as a bird" in her marriage to Thomas.

THE PRIMARY IS BORN

Having spent most of her adolescence caring for her younger siblings, Aurelia now had the opportunity to start her own family. She married Thomas Rogers, a young teamster she had met while crossing the plains, and they settled in Farmington, Utah. When Aurelia started having children, the couple happily welcomed the new little ones into their family. Unfortunately, tragedy came to their doorstep when Aurelia's fourth baby didn't survive infancy. Not only was she overcome with depression, but she also became seriously ill. Aurelia didn't want to die; she knew what it was like to be left motherless at a young age and didn't want her three children to bear the same fate. She prayed constantly, promising that if God would spare her life, she would try to keep His commandments and serve Him to the best of her ability. Aurelia's prayers were answered, and she eventually recovered from her illness. Unfortunately, this wouldn't be the only time death claimed one of Aurelia's babies. Four more of her children died in infancy, leaving Aurelia to mourn and faithfully endure what had befallen her.[6]

Aurelia in her early twenties with her first son, Orson Thomas Rogers

Aurelia loved children. Perhaps because of the loss she had suffered in her own life, she cherished the children around her and knew they were precious in the eyes of Heavenly Father. She found opportunities to honor her promise to God when she saw a group of roguish boys who ran freely through the streets of Farmington. She proposed a Church organization for both boys and girls that would teach them basic principles and values to help them grow into more responsible adults. The Prophet John Taylor liked her idea, and the Primary was born with Aurelia as its leader. At the very first meeting, the children sang, recited poetry, learned the gospel, and participated in activities.[7]

> "Our children are our jewels; we have counted well the cost; May their angels ever guard them, and not one child be lost."
> **AURELIA SPENCER**

In her published autobiography, written years later, Aurelia included the name of every single boy and girl—all 224 of them—who belonged to the first Primary. She felt as though each of those children were her own, and her heart was drawn out with love toward them.[8] The Primary was such a success that within a decade, nearly every Latter-day Saint settlement included a Primary.

EMBRACING THE FUTURE WITH FAITH

Aurelia served on the general board of the Primary organization for the rest of her life.[9] She taught children the sacred principles of the gospel and helped them understand their divine identity, as well as the love their Savior had for them.[10] One might think that such an appointment would have demanded all of Aurelia's time, but she also used her energy to passionately advocate for women's rights. Aurelia was nominated to be one of three Utah delegates to attend the Women's Suffrage Convention in Atlanta, Georgia, as well as the Susan B. Anthony's National Council of Women in Washington, DC.[11]

As a pioneer, wife, mother, Primary leader, and suffragist, Aurelia consistently trusted God's plan for her, even when heartache, uncertainty, and tragedy struck. Before her death in 1922, Aurelia reflected on her life and wrote, "I wish to bear my testimony, that with all that the members of our family have passed through, I have not doubted the truth of the Gospel which I have

Primary general board (clockwise from top left): Aurelia Spencer Rogers, May Anderson, Josephine R. West, Louie B. Felt, and Lillie T. Freeze

embraced, and I feel that I have great cause to be zealous in testifying that I do know that God lives, and that the Church of Jesus Christ of Latter-day Saints is His true Church."[12] No matter her circumstances—be it in the cold and sparsely furnished cabin in Winter Quarters, on the unforgiving terrain across the plains, in her family home in which death was a frequent visitor, or in a gathering of over a hundred bustling children—Aurelia dedicated her life to creating a space where others could be uplifted in love, spiritual safety, and righteousness.

Lilia Wahapaa Kaneihalau

1835–1944

"Mother" to Over Three Hundred Missionaries

"Wherefore, ye must press forward with a steadfastness in Christ, having a perfect brightness of hope, and a love of God and of all men. Wherefore, if ye shall press forward, feasting upon the word of Christ, and endure to the end, behold, thus saith the Father: Ye shall have eternal life." 2 NEPHI 31:20

DEDICATED TO FAMILY AND TRADITIONS

Lilia was born in 1835 to Makaiki and Namu Kaneihalau on the beautiful Hawaiian island of Kauai at a time when grass huts dotted the cliffs, the beating of tapa cloth drummed daily, and whale oil lamps were lit at dusk for light. Like many in Kauai, Lilia and her extended family were very close with one another and with their community. Though Lilia was intimately involved in her parents' home, she lived with her grandparents who lived further down the valley. In their old age, Lilia's grandparents considered her a great help and a treasure.[1]

Lilia and her grandparents lived on the outskirts of the island, carrying on the traditional ways of their Hawaiian ancestors, which meant Lilia didn't socialize very much with people who lived in the local towns. Their lives were bound up in the land, their families, and their church. Instead of attending school, Lilia spent her time helping her grandparents. She fished, prepared food, and took care of the animals. Lilia worked hard on her grandparents' land, a skill that prepared her for a long life of service.[2]

When Lilia was fifteen, she started her first great adventure. Dressed in a fresh tapa skirt and with blossoms in her long dark hair, she traveled on foot with her younger sister to study at a school in Makaweli. Though Lilia was a quiet girl, she excelled in school, learning to read by studying the alphabet, hymns, and the Ten Commandments. She studied at the Makaweli school for six years.

Lilia was also fortunate in that her grandparents faithfully raised her within the wealth of the Kanaka Maoili tradition. At a time when colonization was erasing much of Native Hawaiian culture and the number of Hawaiian language speakers was gradually decreasing, Lilia remained deeply fluent in her Hawaiian culture and language for her whole life.[3]

On December 12, 1850, when Lilia was still a young teenager, ten Latter-day Saint missionaries arrived in Honolulu to spread the gospel in Hawaii. The following day, they climbed a hill that offered a breathtaking view of Honolulu and ocean shorelines. There, they built a stone altar and dedicated the land for missionary work. The missionaries, however, lacked the cultural and language skills necessary to successfully deliver the message of the gospel to Native Hawaiians. White residents also showed no interest in the missionaries' message, and local Protestant ministers tried to deter their work. Additionally, the missionaries had helped spread a deadly smallpox epidemic on the islands, creating a level of disillusionment and distrust among many Hawaiians. Yet there

Lilia was born in 1835, only five years after Joseph Smith organized the restored Church of Jesus Christ. After he died in 1844, she lived another one hundred years before passing away in 1944.

were still eager souls waiting to learn the gospel.[4]

One of these eager souls was Lilia.

"MOTHER WAHAPAA"

While the Utah missionaries soon found success on some islands, such as Maui and Oahu, the work at first seemed futile in the lush and forested valleys of the "Garden Island"—Kauai. After a discouraging thirty days, the elders left the island, and missionaries didn't return for many months.

Lilia with two missionaries

Eventually, Hawaiian missionaries, who had been converted elsewhere, began to teach the Native islanders of Kauai. Because these missionaries were themselves Kanaka Maoli, they understood and respected the people and spoke their language, and they became the first to witness baptisms into the restored Church of Jesus Christ in Kauai.[5] In 1853, one of these missionaries, Elder Kaulaulau, met teenaged Lilia, taught her the gospel, and baptized her at the junction of two rivers near her home.[6] Lilia may have been young, but she had spiritual strength beyond her years as she became one of the earliest and most influential converts to The Church of Jesus Christ of Latter-day Saints in the area.

Lilia was not one to sit by idly while she witnessed the growth of the Church in Hawaii. She dedicated her life to serving and building the kingdom of God with joy. Lilia bore nine children of her own, and raising such a family surely required much time, love, and energy. Yet she also became known as "Mother Wahapaa" to more than three hundred missionaries who served on the islands through the decades. She was revered as a healer; she knew when the missionaries were ailing, lonely, or downcast, and she ministered to their needs by welcoming them into her home.[7] Lilia adored these missionaries, and because of her keen and caring intellect, she could easily recount memories of them too. Whenever she recalled the countless experiences she had with these elders, tears welled up in her eyes, and she beamed with a mother's love.[8]

> Even in her advanced age, Lilia read her small-text Bible every day without the aid of eyeglasses.

Being Mother Wahapaa to missionaries was similar to holding a calling, and Lilia bore this responsibility with pride. In 1893, when she was fifty-eight years old, Lilia was called as the president of her ward's Relief Society. Today Relief Society presidents typically serve for a few years, but this was not the case for Lilia. She served tirelessly for thirty-three years until she was released in 1926 at the age of ninety-one. During her service, she witnessed infant girls become mothers and mothers become grandmothers. She bore a quiet but powerful testimony, taught Sunday School, led spiritual discussions, and served as an example of humility and righteousness.[9]

EMBRACING THE FUTURE WITH FAITH

Lilia lived to be over one hundred years old. Although she lost her hearing and her posture became increasingly stooped with age, Lilia's mind remained as astute as ever, and her zeal for the gospel never diminished.[10] Lilia was the first person to arrive for Church meetings and was the last to leave. The chapel was four miles away from her home, and it could only be reached on foot. Unaccompanied, Lilia walked the four miles to church and the four miles back.[11] This weekly trip required her to shuffle over rocky pathways, skirt along canyon walls, and traverse a rickety bridge that stretched across the Waimea River, the largest river in Kauai. On one terrifying occasion, Lilia fell from the suspension bridge and sustained several painful injuries. But even this accident didn't deter the 103-year-old woman from returning to church a few weeks later. She still made the long journey, only this time, she walked with a pair of crutches.[12]

In 1944, Lilia died at the age of 109, as Hawaii's oldest convert, and she was memorialized as "an enthusiastic spiritual battery that would not quit."[13] During her lifetime, Church membership grew into the thousands, and the Book of

Lilia lived to see the construction of the Laie Hawaii Temple, which was dedicated on November 29, 1919.

Mormon was translated into Hawaiian. Additionally, the first stake in Hawaii was organized on Oahu, and the first temple dedicated outside North America was in Laie.[14] When she was baptized, Lilia couldn't have anticipated the Church's growth in her homeland or her key role in supporting the Lord's work. Through her decades of service and unwavering commitment, she truly was "the noble mother of the Hawaiian Mission."[15]

Annie Gillies
Parker

1847–1905

Faithful Pioneer and Mother to Infamous Outlaw

"And the prayers of the faithful shall be heard, and all those who have dwindled in unbelief shall not be forgotten." 2 NEPHI 26:15

GRIT

In the spring of 1866, Annie gently lifted her first child, a boy, and placed him in the arms of her husband, Max. A circle of men stood at the front of the log church in Beaver, Utah, and Max joined them with his newborn. Annie's father was in the circle, as was her father-in-law, who had traveled over eighty miles by horse and buggy to participate in the special day. Love filled the room as the hope for a new generation poured into the baby. His parents and all four grandparents had immigrated to the United States from England, sacrificing and leaving behind all they knew so their children and grandchildren could hopefully have a better life. Strong hands softly bounced the baby in the center of the circle while he received a name and a blessing. Annie and Max had chosen a strong family name, Robert LeRoy Parker, in honor of both of his grandfathers. Although this is the name that would be written on official Church records, it's not the name Annie's son would be known as by millions of people around the world. They would know him as Butch Cassidy, one of the most infamous outlaws of the Wild West.[1]

Having a child go down a path not only contrary to her desires and beliefs but also contrary to the law of the land was difficult and heartbreaking for Annie. She'd already faced plenty of hardships in her life, but having a child who robbed people at gunpoint? This was a loss at a deeper level, one that only she, as his mother, could feel. Annie would need to face this challenge the way she'd faced others—with faith, determination, and an unbreakable spirit. But could she do it?[2]

Annie's grit had been hard-earned. She was born in England to hardworking Scottish parents. When Church leaders counseled Saints to gather in Utah, Annie's family heeded the call.[3] They packed only their necessary belongings, and as a nine-year-old, Annie boarded a ship for the United States, leaving behind a life that was familiar and comfortable. After arriving in the United States, Annie's family took a train to Iowa, where they joined the Hodgett Wagon Company to travel west alongside the ill-fated Willie Handcart Company. The wagons were full of supplies, making it necessary for Annie to walk the entire 1,200 miles to Salt Lake City. It took over four months, but Annie endured, braving constant hunger and bitter temperatures when early winter storms hit. The ground became so frozen that the pioneer families couldn't dig graves to bury those who succumbed to illness and the harsh conditions. After arriving in Utah, Annie's family eventually settled in Beaver, Utah, where Annie fell in love with and married Max Parker, another English immigrant who had crossed the plains as a child.[4]

Annie's daughter Lula wrote: "I recall how thoughtful my parents were of each other. For example, if Dad was out in the field, Mother would send one of us with a drink of cool water for him. I can still see that shiny brass bucket we carried it in."

Shortly after their marriage, Annie began having babies—and she didn't stop for the next twenty-eight years! She had thirteen children, seven sons and six daughters. To provide for their large family, Annie's husband, Max, often accepted jobs that

took him away from home for long pe-
riods of time. While he was gone, Annie
was left to feed, teach, and discipline the
children on her own in their two-room log
cabin. Although Max eventually stopped
participating in Church activities, Annie
insisted on holding family meetings with
an emphasis on religion and education.
Together they prayed, read from the Book
of Mormon and Bible, and studied pas-

The Parkers' home in Garfield County, Utah, where Annie and Max raised their thirteen children

sages from literature and history. Annie's efforts didn't go unnoticed,
and her children felt the abiding love she had for them. Her daughter Lula Parker Betenson wrote, "There was great love in our home."[5]

A MOTHER'S HEART

With a growing family, Annie and Max bought a ranch and
moved to Circleville, Utah, hoping Max could stay home and farm
the land. But when their crops failed and they lost land to another
homesteader in a property dispute, Max was forced to leave again
to find work. Around this time, a cattle and horse thief named Mike
Cassidy drifted into town. Mike gave Annie's son, Robert, now a
teenager, a saddle and gun and taught him how to shoot, rope, and
brand cattle. Annie didn't like the shady cowboy and warned Robert
about him, but Robert admired Mike and didn't see anything wrong
with their friendship.[6] It wasn't long before Robert started getting
in trouble—first, by stealing a pair of pants, and later by branding
cattle that wasn't his. By the time he was eighteen, he was accused
of stealing a horse.[7] Robert decided it would be best if he left town.
Annie tried to convince him to stay, vowing that she and Max would

help him get out of trouble. Even though Robert adored his mother, he'd become restless in their small town and wanted to leave. After what Annie described as an emotional goodbye, she stared at Robert's back as he rode away, her heart aching. She desperately wanted to shield him from making bad decisions and the unpleasant consequences that might follow. But she also knew most of life's lessons could only be learned through experience. She didn't know that this would be the last time she ever saw her oldest child.

Over the next decade, Annie read about Robert's criminal activities in the newspaper.[8] He robbed banks, trains, and a coal company payroll office, stealing an estimated ten million dollars in today's money. Somewhere along the way, Robert changed his name to Butch Cassidy. Film, literature, and TV have since dramatized his life, making him one of the most well-known icons of the Wild West.[9]

Annie with seven of her children. Leona is on the left; Mark is on horseback; Joseph is in the bassinet; Maximilian has his hand on the horse, standing next to Lula, Annie, and Nina, who is the farthest on the right; Susan is standing in front of her mother.

EMBRACING THE FUTURE WITH FAITH

To help ease the heartache she felt over the path her oldest son had chosen, Annie stayed busy. She cooked and cleaned for her large family. She made her home warm and inviting by singing, making delicious meals, hanging beautiful holiday decorations, and retelling stories from her childhood. Annie's daughter Lula recalled:

"Even though life for the Parkers was a struggle, it was not all work and no play. Our parents' love of fun was passed on to us children. (We) all had good voices, and we enjoyed the bond of music."[10]

Annie also served in her community by regularly feeding her lonely elderly neighbor and by inviting a boy, named Jody Crow, to stay with her family while she doctored his injured leg. Throughout it all, Annie remained a faithful member of the Church. She continued to teach the principles of the gospel to her children and in Sunday School classes at church.

Annie also prayed—mostly about her firstborn son, whom she loved dearly. Her daughter Lula wrote, "If I live to be two hundred, I will always remember Mother's fervent prayers, pleading with God to turn her boy around and bring him home safely, that he might go straight."[11]

As Annie knelt in prayer, perhaps she thought about Robert, her hazel-eyed boy who loved animals and playing make-believe with his younger siblings. Or maybe she reminisced about the poplar trees he'd helped her plant along their property's edge or the way he'd lifted her off her feet when he squeezed her in a tight hug. Hopefully, in return, Heavenly Father whispered to her heart that she was a good mom because she had valiantly given her all and that, no matter what choices her son made, she was a righteous mother because she'd never stopped loving, thinking about, or praying for her son. Because at the end of each day, praying was the most-powerful thing Annie could do.[12] The rest was in the Lord's hands.

At the age of fifty-seven, Annie died peacefully in her sleep due to heart problems. Her daughter Lula said, "Mother's death was a great shock to the whole family. She had always made the best of things and looked on the bright side, and we couldn't reconcile ourselves to being without her at first. We lacked the great faith she possessed. For many days Dad walked all the way out to the ranch and back to wear out his grief."

Martha Ann
Stevens Howell

1875–1954

Missionary Who Persevered through Prejudice in the Church

"He inviteth them all to come unto him and partake of his goodness; and he denieth none that come unto him, black and white, bond and free, male and female." 2 NEPHI 26:33

AN EXTRAORDINARY CALL

In 1951, Martha Ann and her husband, Abner, were called to serve an extraordinary mission, one that was never again duplicated. For much of the Church's history, from the mid-1800s until 1978, the Church did not ordain men of black African descent to its priesthood or allow Black men or women to participate in temple endowment or sealing ordinances. This helped reinforce the racial inequity and oppression already present among Church members in the nineteenth century. Because of this, it was difficult for many Black individuals to feel a sense of belonging among the Latter-day Saints, and Church leaders were concerned that very few descendants of Black pioneers had stayed active in the Church. Simultaneously, they observed that other Christian denominations, including the Methodists and Baptists, had successfully established Black congregations. The practice of segregation was common in the United States in the 1950s, and though the Church had

When Martha Ann was a young mom, her dear friend Nettie died from a heart condition. Martha Ann took in Nettie's two daughters and raised them as her own until their father remarried.

never had a policy of segregated congregations, leaders wondered if Black Latter-day Saints would be interested in something similar. They called Martha Ann and Abner, both Black Latter-day Saints, to serve in the Southern and Eastern states to assess the needs of Black Church members and to investigate the possibility of establishing Black congregations.[1]

Martha Ann and Abner were perfectly suited for this mission. They were known for their friendliness, work ethic, and strong testimonies of the gospel. Both had been harmed by racism, and Martha Ann had a deep desire to change such prejudices.[2] Before moving to Utah, Abner's parents had been enslaved, and Martha Ann had been born in 1875, just ten years after the Civil War had ended. Martha Ann's family was well known and respected in the Salt Lake Valley. She was named after her maternal grandmother, Martha Vilate Flake, who had been enslaved and migrated to the West with the Mississippi Saints. Martha Ann's grandfather Green Flake had been baptized and came across the plains, while still enslaved, with the very first pioneer company in 1847. He was among the first to enter the Salt Lake Valley and was among those who heard Brigham Young

Martha Ann Stevens (left) with her mother, Lucinda Flake Stevens (center), and sister Mary Belle Stevens Oglesby, circa 1900

say, "This is the right place." Green and Martha Vilate were married in Salt Lake City after Green had paid Martha's enslaver for her freedom. Both Green and Martha had faith in God's plan, and upon Green's death, a newspaper wrote that he had "always remained a firm believer in the Mormon faith."[3]

Although Martha Ann's family descended from the same group of hardworking pioneers as White Latter-day Saints, some Church members had discriminated against her mother because of her skin color and declared they wouldn't attend services if a Black person was present. Because of this racial discrimination, Martha Ann's mom quit attending church meetings. Amid such racism and abuse, Martha Ann, and a handful of other descendants of Black pioneers, still chose to remain active in the Church.[4]

> Martha Ann loved to read and cared deeply about literacy. Martha Ann's daughter, Mary Lucille Bankhead, said: "Every night, we read something. After dinner was over with and the dishes and everything were done, we read. Mother insisted on it."

HE INVITETH ALL TO PARTAKE

When Martha Ann and Abner left on their mission to the Southern and Eastern states, the presiding bishop of the Church, LeGrand Richards, wrote a letter for them to present to the congregations they visited. Because of common discriminatory attitudes in the Church and throughout the United States, it's likely that some Latter-day Saint congregations would have been wary or unwelcoming of the Black couple; the letter introduced the Howells and assured Church members that the Howells were there on a Church-sanctioned mission. Richards explained that they had been asked to call upon the missionaries and Saints in the area and requested that the members accept the Howells with kindness and courtesy.

After visiting the Eastern states, Martha Ann and Abner traveled to Cincinnati, Ohio, where they met Len and Mary Hope. Martha Ann and Mary became fast friends. They were about the same age, and both were Black Latter-day Saint women. They understood what it was like to be disenfranchised and to experience racism within their chosen faith. The local branch president forbade the Hope family from attending the all-White Church meetings in Cincinnati. Despite feeling the pain of rejection, they met with the missionaries monthly in their home.[5] Reflecting upon the Hope family's situation, Abner said: "We found that society had creeped into religion. Most of the members lived across the river on the Kentucky side, and some of them did not want the Negro family to come to church."[6]

Martha Ann with her husband, Abner

That Sunday, the Howells and Hopes attended the Cincinnati branch. They presented LeGrand Richards's letter, and Abner was invited to speak. In his remarks, Abner shared 2 Nephi 26:33, which reads: "He inviteth them all to come unto him and partake of his goodness; and he denieth none that come unto him, black and white, bond and free, male and female." After the meeting, members of the congregation approached Abner and Martha Ann and shook their hands. One man said, "I didn't know there were such things in the Book of Mormon."[7]

At the end of their mission, Martha Ann and Abner concluded that segregated branches weren't a sustainable option for the Church because of the small number of Black Latter-day Saints. Other Black Christian congregations were flourishing in the United States, but prejudice and false beliefs among the Latter-day Saints regarding people of African descent stymied the spread of the gospel among Black Americans.[8] Although their mission wasn't to preach, Martha Ann and Abner bravely stood up against such prejudice and taught gospel truths.

EMBRACING THE FUTURE WITH FAITH

Martha Ann lived during a unique time in United States history—she was born shortly after slavery had been abolished and passed away just before the beginning of the Civil Rights Movement. In childhood, she was close with her grandparents, who told her stories of their enslavement.[9] Martha Ann passed away on May 10, 1954, and exactly one week later, after years of political activism from many Black Americans, the US Supreme Court outlawed segregation in schools.

Martha Ann stood with poise and purpose as a Black member of the Church. She sought for all to receive an education, had a gift for making friends easily, and raised

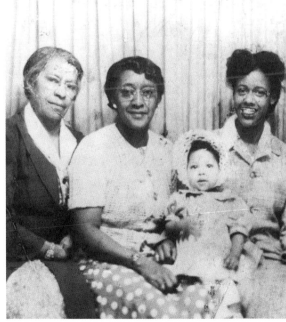

Four generations. From left to right: Martha Ann Stevens Howell, Mary Lucille Bankhead, Juanita Spillman (child), and Ruth Jackson

her family in the faith despite the racism in the Church.[10] Martha Ann's daughter, Mary Lucille Bankhead, became the first Relief Society president of the Genesis Group, an organization created by Church leaders in 1971 to support and meet the needs of Black Latter-day Saints.[11] Martha Ann's posterity, along with many others, were affected for good by her testimony and her strength in her beliefs.[12]

THE GENESIS GROUP

In 1971, three Black Latter-day Saints—Ruffin Bridgeforth, Darius Gray, and Eugene Orr—partnered together to garner more support for Black members of the Church. They expressed concern about the Church's position on Black Latter-day Saints with President Joseph Fielding Smith. In response, the prophet asked then-Apostles Gordon B. Hinckley, Thomas S. Monson, and Boyd K. Packer to meet

with these men. Consequently, on October 19, 1971, the Genesis Group was founded to focus on the needs of Black Latter-day Saints.[13] Darius Gray said, "Genesis was, and is, a unique unit of the Church. We are like no other Church organization but our existence was brought into being by the direct actions of the First Presidency and the Quorum of the Twelve."[14]

Ruffin Bridgeforth, the first president of the original Genesis Group, with then-Elder Gordon B. Hinckley of the Quorum of the Twelve Apostles at a meeting in 1971

The Genesis Group provides opportunities for fellowship, organizes devotionals and activities, and welcomes Black Latter-day Saints in an affirming environment. Group meetings often include a gospel choir as well as call-and-response testimonies.[15] In 2021, the Genesis Group celebrated its fifty-year anniversary and continues to support thousands of individuals by fostering an accepting community where they can celebrate their collective identity. The president of the group since 2018, Davis Stovall, said: "And that is what Genesis is about. We celebrate our spiritual identity, which is our cultural identity. We put the Lord and Savior Jesus Christ first."[16]

Auguste
Kuhlmann Lippelt

1880–1952

Convert Who Shared the Gospel in Brazil

"I [will] bring forth my word unto the children of men, yea, even upon all the nations of the earth." **2 NEPHI 29:7**

A DYING SON'S VISION

Life was hard for many families living in Germany after World War I. Their country was in debt, their money had become useless, and there was a nationwide food shortage.[1] Auguste and her husband, Robert, were raising seven children in these difficult circumstances, and they faced additional heartache when their ten-year-old son became gravely ill. As he lay in bed on the verge of death, he had a vision. He told his older sister about it when she came into the room: "Here in this room," he said, "just a bit ago were our grandparents, who said to me that next Thursday, at this hour, they will come get me, and I will be dying. . . . And on the Sunday after my death, when you are going to church, a woman will invite you to attend her church with her. And this other church is the one to which our grandparents want you to belong."[2]

Events unfolded exactly as Auguste's son had envisioned. He passed away the following Thursday, and three days later, as the Lippelt children walked to their Protestant church, they met a woman named Sister Demmel. She invited them to her church—The Church of Jesus Christ of Latter-day Saints. Remembering the words of their brother, the children accompanied her. A few months later, Auguste and her four oldest children were baptized.[3] Despite his son's vision, Auguste's husband, Robert, was very unhappy about his family's newfound faith. He didn't believe in God and had no desire to learn about the gospel.

"HERE THE MORMONS WILL NOT FIND ME"

Auguste and Robert struggled to feed their children in post-war Germany. Robert, a professional painter and dance instructor, thought he might find better work opportunities if they left the country. But he also had another motive for moving—he wanted to take his family as far away from the Church as possible. He searched for places where the Church didn't exist. He thought Brazil, which was all the way across the world—nearly six thousand miles away—was the answer. But he didn't think through the repercussions of taking five of the Church's newest and most eager members with him.

Robert moved his family to a small village called Ipoméia in the south of Brazil. "Here the Mormons will not find me," he reasoned.[4] Although the Church was absent in Brazil, Robert's wife was very much present. Undeterred by her husband's disapproval, Auguste shared her strong testimony of the gospel with

Auguste (center front) with her husband and family

her neighbors and wrote to the prophet, Heber J. Grant, in Salt Lake, requesting for missionaries and teaching materials to be sent to Brazil—especially to her town of Ipoméia. Missionary work thrived in the little village because Auguste became God's instrument in sharing the good news of the gospel with other German immigrants in the area. But even though Auguste held Church meetings in her

Auguste and Robert

home, her husband continued to distance himself from his wife's faith.

On Christmas morning in 1925, all South American countries, including Brazil, were dedicated for missionary work. Because Auguste had sent letters to Church leaders, the mission president visited her. He witnessed the great work she had done and assigned missionaries to Ipoméia. Their first order of business was to create the Ipoméia Branch so they could build upon the strong foundation Auguste had established among other Caucasian settlers in that area. Initially, the missionaries mainly preached the gospel to German immigrants, who were among some of the first converts in Brazil.[5] It unfortunately took another thirteen years before Church meetings were held in Brazil's official language of Portuguese. But once this happened, the gospel flourished among the Brazilian people, and the Church grew faster in Brazil than in any other South American country.[6]

Because of the growth in Ipoméia, a Latter-day Saint chapel was constructed in the small village.[7] But despite Auguste's tremendous success in laying groundwork and spreading the gospel, there was someone very dear to her who still hadn't joined the Church when she died in 1952 at the age of seventy-two.[8]

EMBRACING THE FUTURE WITH FAITH

Several years after Auguste died, her husband, Robert, suffered a stroke and became partially paralyzed. He moved in with his daughter, who purposely left Church books close to his newspapers. He secretly began reading the Book of Mormon, and his heart softened. One day he announced, "I want to go where my wife is." After meeting with the missionaries, Robert accepted the gospel. Because of his paralysis, some worried that it might be dangerous for Robert to enter the waters of baptism, but he had faith. "I am sure that through the infinite kindness of the Lord, I shall walk out of the water completely healed," he assured them. On the day of his baptism, he was carried to the Rio de Peixe. After he was baptized, a miracle occurred. He walked unassisted out of the river and remained a faithful member of the Church for the rest of his life.[9]

Fittingly, the name *Ipoméia* means "morning glory," a plant whose flowers are shaped in the form of a trumpet, an instrument that symbolizes the declaration of important news. Like a trumpet, Auguste was God's instrument in declaring the good news of the gospel.

Even though Auguste's husband had moved her far from her homeland after her conversion, she persevered in Brazil by holding family prayer, leading family home evenings, and holding study meetings in her home.[10] Her hard work was fundamental in helping the Church to arrive when and where it did. Nearly one hundred years after missionaries first preached in South America, Brazil had 1,429,935 members, thirty-five missions, and seven temples. To this day, Auguste is considered a faithful pioneer in the Ipoméia region of Brazil.[11]

EARLY FEMALE CONVERTS IN BRAZIL

When dedicating the Ipoméia chapel, President Spencer W. Kimball referred to the crucial role of mothers in furthering the Church's progress. He said, "The hand that rocks the cradle governs the world."[12] Women truly were great pioneers in Brazil. At the end of 1934, Auguste was one of 132 women in the South American Mission affiliated with the Church. There were only fifty-seven men (only one of whom had been ordained an elder) and fifty-two children. Relief Society and Primary, both organizations led by women, were the strongest auxiliaries of the era. "The importance of the old manuals, holding family home evening, family prayer, all of this was fundamental in helping the Church to arrive where it did and much of that is due to the mothers," remembers Norma Halter, who was one of the fifty-two children attending Church in South America during that time.[13]

Geraldine Bangerter, bottom left, with Brazilian sisters Greta Kearns, Julieta Ardito, and Luci Barbieri, who helped establish Relief Society in their homeland

Irene Colvin Corbett

1881–1912

Nurse and Passenger on the *Titanic*

"When ye are in the service of your fellow beings ye are only in the service of your God." MOSIAH 2:17

A DESIRE TO SERVE

No one knows exactly what Irene was doing when the *Titanic*'s barely used china came crashing to the floor or when ice-cold saltwater rushed down the ship's pristine hallways. While passengers with third-class tickets were held back from boarding the inadequate supply of lifeboats, those with second-class tickets were encouraged to board. As a result, 93 percent of the women and children from upper-deck cabins boarded the lifeboats, but Irene, who possessed a second-class ticket, wasn't among them.[1]

Six months earlier, Irene had sailed to Great Britain to study midwifery at General Lying-In Hospital in London, one of the first maternity hospitals in England. Irene was smart and ambitious. As a suffragist, she believed women deserved just as many rights as men did. This belief, along with her life-long desire to serve others, may have been

Irene as a child

As the oldest of six children, Irene helped care for her younger siblings on the family farm. They all admired and looked up to her.

what prompted her to pursue a vocation and to develop and hone her skills as a nurse. Doctors at the local hospital in Provo, Utah, had witnessed Irene's talent and compassion when she assisted them with births. Because the infant deathrate in her hometown of Provo was high, they encouraged her to study in London, knowing that the advanced medical knowledge she would obtain there would save lives in their rural community.

For Irene, however, the decision to pursue medical training in London was extremely difficult because she would have to leave her husband, Walter, and their three small children. Her husband

didn't want her to go, but after much thought and prayer, Irene finally decided to make the journey. With her parents' support (they cared for her children and mortgaged their farm to help pay for her education and travel), Irene sailed to Great Britain on the reverse course of her pioneer grandmother who had immigrated to Utah from England.[2]

While in London, Irene achieved top marks in her nursing classes. On weekends, she often ministered to sick children in the city's slums and gave money to their mothers. After completing the program, Irene longed for her family and wanted to return home as

The graduating midwife-nursing class from London's General Lying-In Hospital. Irene is at the top of the photo because she was at the top of the class.

quickly as possible. In a letter to her sister, Irene wrote a few words about her youngest son: "Can just hear little Mack. How I do love that baby."[3]

THE WORLD'S MOST FAMOUS OCEAN CATASTROPHE

Before marrying Walter, Irene was a dedicated and revered teacher at the Peteetneet Academy in Payson, Utah.

For thirteen pounds—only seventeen US dollars—Irene purchased a second-class ticket aboard the *Titanic*, a brand-new luxury liner that had been deemed "unsinkable."[4] Irene had experienced a terrifying voyage on her way to England. She had crossed the Atlantic during a severe winter storm on the *Virginian*, a small, single-funnel steamship. According to her grandson, who owns most of her surviving letters and postcards, Irene booked passage aboard the *Titanic* to avoid a similar journey on the way home. He said Irene was also "excited to have missionaries making the trip with her" on the *Titanic*.[5] Having missionaries aboard a ship was considered a good omen, not only by Church members but also by sea captains. But unbeknownst to Irene, the six missionaries had rebooked passage on a different ship for the following day.

When Irene's family learned that the ship had sunk and heard that the missionaries had rebooked on a different ship, they held onto hope that she'd done the same. But a few days after the sinking of the *Titanic*, they received a telegram confirming that Irene had

Irene with her one-year-old son, Mack

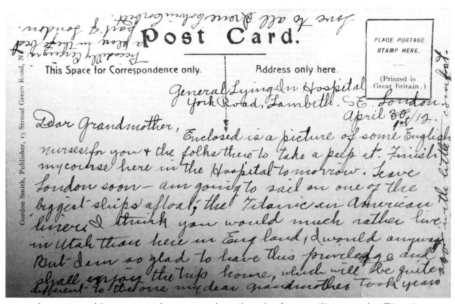

A postcard Irene sent her grandmother before sailing on the Titanic

been one of the 2,224 passengers aboard the ship but not one of the 711 survivors. Her family was devastated. Irene had been close with her supportive father, and it was said that when he heard she had drowned, it was as if his hair turned white overnight. Irene's letters brought sadness rather than comfort to her mother, so in an attempt to ease their mother's grief, Irene's sister destroyed most of Irene's papers and letters.[6]

EMBRACING THE FUTURE WITH FAITH

Although she lived for only thirty years, Irene left an immeasurable impact on those around her. She embarked on an adventure of service and learning, hoping it would allow her to better serve her community. She missed her family terribly while she was away in London, but she was very dedicated to her medical training. Irene was one among several women who studied mid-wifery and brought down the infant deathrate in their communities. After learning of Irene's death, the nurses who had worked with her in London sent a letter to her family, describing how they all had loved Irene and would miss her dearly.[7] The final hours of Irene's life will remain a mystery, but we do know she was brave, compassionate, prayerful, and valiant.

The *Titanic* sent out distress calls while it was sinking. One of the ships to answer the call and start steaming toward the *Titanic* was the *Virginian*, the ship on which Irene had traveled to England. Her horrible crossing on the *Virginian* was one of the reasons Irene booked returning passage on a much larger ship.

Helen Dowawisnima
Sekaquaptewa

1898–1991

Leader Who Bridged Two Cultures

"Verily I say unto you, Inasmuch as ye have done it unto one of the least of these my brethren, ye have done it unto me." **MATTHEW 25:40**

TAKEN BY FORCE

In 1906, when Helen was seven years old, she and her family awoke one morning to find United States military troops surrounding their adobe home. The soldiers were there to take Helen.[1] Helen's parents had spent their lives on their Hopi ancestral lands in Oraibi, Arizona, and had resisted sending their daughter to the government-owned boarding school, which was a two days' walk from their village. United States officials had built the school to teach Hopi children the ways of White settler life. At the school, children were forced not only to live away from their homes and families but also to give up their Hopi language, their clothing, and even their names. Some Hopi parents chose to let their children attend the school, believing that their lives could be easier if they assimilated into the dominant, American culture. Others, however, like Helen's parents, wanted their children to live at home and be educated in the Hopi tradition. Helen's parents educated her through on-the-job training. She worked beside them, learning how to raise corn, prepare food, care for sheep, and maintain a household. When parents refused to send their children to the boarding school, the military was sent to take them by force.[2]

Helen's parents watched helplessly, and in great pain, as the soldiers loaded Helen and eighty-one other Hopi children into wagons and carted them off to Keams Canyon Boarding School. When Helen arrived at the school, everything felt foreign. She was given new clothes, food she'd never eaten, and a double bed to share with two other girls. Helen's parents had named her Dowawisnima, meaning "a trail marked by sand," but she was renamed "Helen" by White teachers. The school had electric lights, something entirely new to Helen; she grew up utilizing natural light and resources. After the sun went down and the lights stayed on, she was so confused that she thought it was still daytime. It disrupted the natural rhythm her traditional upbringing had accustomed her to.[3]

Hopi women outside their traditional Hopi homes, circa 1906

Helen remained at Keams Canyon Boarding School for the next thirteen years. During this time, she learned the English language and gained a desire to learn about the Western culture. She believed there were benefits to a Western approach to education but also experienced a great deal of injustice and prejudice at the boarding school. She was often hungry, which made it difficult to sleep. When she was homesick, she'd cry in a corner so she wouldn't be heard and scolded or spanked. Once while in class, after she gave the wrong answer, the teacher slapped her ear, giving her a prolonged earache. Helen had a hard time hearing out of that ear even as an adult.[4]

Helen eventually chose to combine both ways of life. She had a great respect for her Hopi upbringing, the wise philosophies she learned from her parents, and the lack of worldliness on the reservation. Helen never forgot the abuse she and other students had suffered at the boarding schools, but she came to appreciate the Western approach to medicine and the knowledge she gained through reading English, and she even preferred the cotton dresses to the wool ones her family had worn. Helen determined to integrate the very best of the two worlds into her life.[5]

LIVING TWO CULTURES

While attending Keams Canyon Boarding School, Helen admired a Hopi upperclassman named Emory from afar. One evening he delivered a package to her from her mother. Her face lit up when she saw him, and he stayed awhile so they could talk. Helen later wrote, "Emory has been the light in my life ever since."[6]

Helen and Emory married and had ten children and also raised two foster sons. They settled on the Hopi reservation, their lives a combination of both ways of life—the Hopi way mixed with what she and Emory had learned at school. Their children learned from nature but also attended the government's day school. Helen made her own medicine out of native plants to clear up sores, colds, and coughs but also

In her autobiography, Helen wrote, "Once I had washed and ironed some clothes for a woman who was sick. When I went to deliver them to her little boy—the rascal—said, 'You look like a witch.' [My husband] Emory said, 'She is one of the best witches we have. Always helping people.'"

had her children immunized against life-threatening diseases like smallpox and diphtheria. Helen gave birth to each of her children at home just like her mother and grandmothers had done, but when one of her babies, Wayne, became extremely ill, she took him to the Western hospital. At the time, many Hopi were wary of hospitals because their community had been historically mistreated in such places, but Helen made her own choice. Wayne stayed in the hospital for six months, and Helen felt he would've died if it weren't for the medical attention he received there.[7]

Living both ways of life wasn't always easy for Helen and her family. When she and Emory didn't do things according to Hopi tradition, they were met with distrust by some neighbors. Others in Helen's village—especially her father—didn't like that she enjoyed reading Western books or that she had a desire for her children to be successful in Western schools. Eventually, Helen and Emory decided it would be best for them to move off the reservation and away from mistrusting neighbors. They settled on a ranch in a two-room rock house, in which the hillside served as the main wall. Though she missed her community, they were happy there; they planted an orchard, raised corn for their growing family, started a cattle business, and made friends with those who passed by. Helen told travelers that if they came upon her family's home while they were away, they should eat their food—and even sleep in their beds—until she and her family returned.[8]

Eventually, the fracture between Helen and the people in her village began to mend. She admitted that she had been as reluctant about returning to some of the Hopi ways as they had been about adopting aspects of Western culture. Helen said that "a spirit of tolerance . . . gradually replaced a spirit of hostility."[9]

In 1951, Helen was introduced to The Church of Jesus Christ of Latter-day Saints by the first full-time missionaries, a senior couple, in Oraibi. Many of the Church's teachings made sense to Helen and coincided with Hopi beliefs. While Helen was growing up, Helen's father had instructed her to forgive, serve others, and share with those in need. Her mother had taught her the Hopi moral code, which was to keep herself morally clean before marriage and to be true to her husband after she was married. Like Latter-day Saints, Hopis believe in eternal marriage. When she and Emory read the Book of Mormon, they believed it to be true because it sounded like a familiar story and reminded them of Hopi tradition. After studying the gospel for two years, Helen and two of her children were baptized by her son Wayne, who had been converted in Phoenix. About becoming a Latter-day Saint, Helen wrote, "I have no doubt I did right. I have never been sorry. It has made a better woman of me, and I have surely been happy in my church. I have had great satisfaction working in the church, even though it seemed like everything was against me at times."[10]

Nurtured by her Hopi upbringing, Helen's nature was to help people who were poor, sick, or hungry. She loved relieving them and credited the Church's Relief Society organization for truly showing her how to minister like the Savior. For fifteen years she served as the Relief Society president

The main street of Oraibi, Helen's village, circa 1899

of the Oraibi area. She walked for miles to minister to others, teach homemaking skills, and uplift the Hopi women. Her charm, wisdom, and cheerful laugh helped her win the hearts of those she served.[11]

EMBRACING THE FUTURE WITH FAITH

Although small in stature, Helen had an indomitable spirit and was described as living a life "marked by milestones of progress, goals of achievement, and landmarks to inspire her people."[12] She loved and respected her people's way of life but also implemented the ideas and practices from American culture that she believed could help her family. Many of her children and grandchildren contributed

Helen shucking corn, 1980. Corn is central to Hopi culture, religion, and way of life.

significantly to the growth and development of the Hopi people. Among her children were educators, police officers, and a social worker. One son, who owned a jewelry store employing Hopi men, and her daughter, Marlene, sat on the tribal council.[13]

At the end of her life, Helen said, "Most people who are as old as Emory and I have better houses and furniture than we do. We sacrificed so we could invest our money in our children."

With her charming personality and willingness to share her life story, Helen became a well-known spokesperson for her tribe. She was happy to explain the Hopi culture, give her insights and impressions of the Western culture, and share her faith. She wrote a book entitled Me and Mine, in which she preserved her fascinating history for future generations. Her book was considered unique because very few Hopi women wrote down their stories. As such, it was a valuable contribution to the recorded history of Indigenous peoples and was used as a textbook in high school and college classrooms throughout the United States.[14] Helen also served as the chief matriarch of the Hopi tribe, and, in 2013, she was inducted into the Arizona Women's Hall of Fame.

After years of grief and feeling rejected over Helen's choice to adopt so many Western ways, Helen's father died at age ninety-five, but not before acknowledging that Helen's choices had been right for her. He'd once viewed her as a radical, but he finally saw her as a guardian and preserver of the Hopi tradition.[15]

Maxine Tate Grimm

1914–2017

Musician Who Shared the Gospel in Southeast Asia

"If thou art merry, praise the Lord with singing, with music, with dancing, and with a prayer of praise and thanksgiving." **D&C 136:28**

THE GIFT OF MUSIC

As a child, Maxine often drifted to sleep at night listening to the melodies that her mother played on the piano. Those nightly lullabies instilled a great love of music in Maxine, and from a young age, she grew to be a gifted musician. She enjoyed sharing her talent with others and even played the piano for Tooele High School's musical productions.[1] After her mother died from a rare blood disorder, Maxine soothed her deep sorrow by playing the piano.[2] She lived and breathed music; it reminded her of her mother and brought comfort in times of distress. But she couldn't imagine the profound influence music would continue to have on her life as well as the lives of others. In her patriarchal blessing, she was promised that she would do great good with her gift of music.

Maxine with her portable organ during World War II

Maxine earned a bachelor's degree in textiles with four minors and a master's degree from New York University, and she attended flight school.

When Maxine was in her mid-twenties, World War II broke out, and the world was in turmoil. Maxine also experienced her own personal turmoil when her high school sweetheart and husband, Veldon Shields, died of an unknown sickness, just seven months into their marriage. Despite this devastating loss, Maxine signed up to serve in the American Red Cross in order to help others and spread the gospel.[3] She was sent to Southeast Asia to support, encourage, and boost the morale of injured soldiers. While overseas, Maxine worked in the military hospital's psychiatric ward, and her gift for music blessed the lives of countless soldiers. She played the piano, sang, and used her well-traveled army field pump organ to spread joy, hope, and the beautiful hymns of the gospel.[4]

Maxine with her husband, Pete

CARRYING ZION WITH HER

Although Maxine felt closer to God when she played sacred hymns, she still longed to attend church and wished she could meet with fellow Saints to take the sacrament. Pete Grimm, an army colonel she'd been dating, although not a Latter-day Saint himself, offered his home as a place for Maxine and three servicemen to gather. Maxine felt overwhelmed by the opportunity to worship with others. During their first meeting, her tears splashed on the organ keys as she played "Come, Come, Ye Saints." News about the service spread, and the following Sunday, at least ten more servicemen attended the meeting.[5]

Maxine recognized the power of meeting as a congregation, and she carried her love for the gospel wherever she went. When the war ended, the American Red Cross sent Maxine to Japan for two years to be the recreation director for all hospitals. She found Latter-day Saints who had been baptized before the war and invited them to attend church meetings. But Maxine didn't stop there. After she married Pete Grimm and settled in the Philippines, she organized Primary and Sunday School meetings. She loved the Filipino

In the Philippines, the Grimms had a mini zoo at their home, complete with monkeys, birds, and other animals. Their many visitors played volleyball on their grassy lawn and swam in their pool.

Attending church in the Philippines. Aniceta Fajardo, the first Filipino convert, is on the first row, second person from the left; Maxine is the fifth person from the left.

A baptismal service in the pool at the home of Maxine and Pete Grimm, circa 1964

Maxine's son, Pete Jr., recalls about his mom, "She had a great memory until her final few years. And even after she had forgotten her own name, she could still play the organ and knew the words to 40s hit songs. . . . The power of music was always a major factor in her life."

people and had a deep desire for the Church to be officially established in the Philippines. She did her best to teach the gospel and was unceasing in her pleas for missionaries to be sent to the country.[6]

Permission was finally given for the Church to enter the Philippines. On June 6, 1961, four missionaries arrived, ready to preach the gospel. Maxine and Pete became the unofficial "mom and dad" of the mission, and some of the first converts in the Philippines—two thousand of them—were baptized in the Grimms' swimming pool. Maxine and Pete worked tirelessly to spread the gospel in the Philippines. Though still not a member of the Church, Maxine's husband assisted her every step of the way. Maxine always told people Pete would join when he was ready.[7] And when he finally was, someone very special baptized him: his son, Pete Jr.[8]

EMBRACING THE FUTURE WITH FAITH

Maxine grew up in the small railway town of Tooele, Utah, but she traveled across the world, bringing nothing but a few possessions, her musical talents, and her testimony.[9] Her music comforted those she interacted with and helped people gather together to worship, to heal, and to witness her passion for the gospel. By the time Maxine passed away at the age of 102, Church membership in the

Philippines had reached over 800,000.[10] Maxine never bore the official missionary nametag, but she helped The Church of Jesus Christ of Latter-day Saints flourish wherever she went—all because she had a love of God, a desire to serve, and a little portable organ.[11]

As of November 2022, the Philippines had two operating temples, four under construction, and four announced.

ANICETA FAJARDO

THE FIRST FILIPINO CONVERT

Toward the end of World War II, the Red Cross assigned Maxine to care for prisoners of war in the Philippines and organize a camp for refugees. It was here that she met and became friends with Aniceta, a Filipino seamstress working at the camp.[12] Aniceta wanted to be baptized, but Church leaders were hesitant to baptize new converts in the Philippines without a plan for supporting the new members. There were no missionaries in the country, and the only Church meetings were those organized by Maxine. However, special permission was finally given, and in 1945, Aniceta was the first Filipino to be baptized in the Philippines. The next Filipino convert, David Lagman, was not baptized until 1958, thirteen years later.[13]

Aniceta Pabilona Fajardo, the first convert in the Philippines

Carmen Galvez O'Donnal

1922–1998

Problem-Solver Who Changed How the Saints Learn and Worship

"For behold, thus saith the Lord God: I will give unto the children of men line upon line, precept upon precept, here a little and there a little; . . . for unto him that receiveth I will give more." **2 NEPHI 28:30**

"ETERNAL LOVE AFFAIR"

Nineteen-year-old Carmen was playing Ping-Pong at a local tennis club when her friend called her over to a table because a *gringo* wanted to talk to her. "Since when does a lady have to go to meet a gentleman?" she replied. "If he wants to meet me, he will have to come over here."[1] The gringo was John O'Donnal, an American working in Guatemala as an agricultural advisor for the United States, and he spoke perfect Spanish. When he heard Carmen's response, he approached the spunky dark-haired woman, and replied in Spanish, "Where in the world have you been?"[2]

After this introduction, it took only two months for Carmen and John to fall in love.

Carmen and John on their wedding day

Carmen with her parents at the coffee farm where John asked for their consent to marry Carmen

But because John was a Latter-day Saint, Carmen's devout Catholic family and friends weren't happy about their relationship. The two almost broke up, but John said there was "a strong, unseen influence urging us on," and they decided to get married.[3] After discussing their plans with Carmen's mom, all three of them drove two hours to a farm where Carmen's dad was working to ask for his permission to be married. The four openly considered the problems that Carmen and John might face having been raised in different cultures and religions. But in the end, Carmen's parents were open minded and gave their full consent and blessing. John and Carmen were married on June 19, 1943, at the club where they first met. This marked the beginning of what John described as "a beautiful, eternal love affair."[4]

Carmen admired her husband's strong devotion and love for the gospel. He frequently told her how he wished the people of Guatemala could learn more about his faith.[5] Little did he know his wife would be the driving force behind making his wishes come true.

WISHES GRANTED

On a trip to Salt Lake City in 1946, John visited the prophet, George Albert Smith, and personally asked him if the Church would send missionaries to Guatemala. His plea was heard, and a little over a year later Central America was dedicated for the preaching of the gospel. The O'Donnals invited the first Central American missionaries to live in an upstairs room in their home.

Carmen was determined to learn more about the church her husband loved. She obtained a Spanish copy of the Book of Mormon but found the words and stories difficult to understand. "It doesn't mean anything to me," she complained.[6] John promised her that if she would continue to read and pray, eventually understanding would come.

One evening when John was away, Carmen studied the Book of Mormon. As she began to pray, a dark presence surrounded her. Her immediate thought was "For some reason, Satan is trying to destroy me in this."[7] She ran to the room of the missionaries who were living in her home and begged for help. They gave her a priesthood blessing, which calmed her fears and gave her courage to move forward with her desire to learn about the gospel.

Carmen was baptized by her husband, John, in November 1948

After five years of carefully studying the scriptures, Carmen said she finally gained a testimony.[8] On a sunny November morning in 1948, John baptized Carmen in a private pool in Vista Hermosa, making her the first Central American convert. "It was a beautiful day," John remembered later. "I was so happy to be the one to baptize the first member and even happier that it was my wife."[9]

The following month, Carmen was called to be the Relief Society president of Central America—all seven countries! She soon noticed how complicated it was

Carmen served as the first temple matron of the Guatemala City Guatemala Temple.

Carmen's daughter-in-law, Elena Von-Esh O'Donnal, says she started investigating the Church because when she'd visit Carmen's home, she felt a strong, peaceful spirit. Elena wanted to know the Heavenly Father that Carmen so strongly believed in. Elena was baptized at eighteen, and she believes her children (Carmen's grandchildren) chose to serve missions because of Carmen's love and example.

for those who had limited experience in the Church to understand the Sunday School lessons, which often used unfamiliar jargon and stories. To solve this problem, she developed and taught adjusted lessons that focused on essential gospel principles to new members and investigators. A visiting General Authority sat in on one of her lessons and observed its effectiveness. His observation led the Church to adopt a new Sunday School class called Gospel Principles. This program benefited the Church and members worldwide.

Carmen wasn't done observing and seeking solutions in behalf of Church members in Guatemala. Many of them had to walk on dusty roads for hours or take bumpy, overcrowded buses to their church buildings. In addition, church meetings were spread throughout the day and week, so those long journeys took place more than just once on Sundays. The O'Donnals, and particularly Carmen, understood the needs of Central American Saints, and they had two suggestions: First, change the Sunday meetings to a consolidated meeting block—a schedule in which all meetings were held one right after another instead of at different times throughout the day or week. And second, build more meetinghouses so Latter-day Saints would not have to travel so far to attend church. Church leaders listened to these ideas and piloted the first consolidated meeting block in Guatemala City. And when they began constructing smaller, less-expensive local meetinghouses in Guatemala, the Church had the O'Donnals oversee the project. Both of these pioneering ideas were later adopted Churchwide.[10]

EMBRACING THE FUTURE WITH FAITH

Carmen's leap of faith into the waters of baptism set a precedent for generations of Central Americans who would follow. She was described as a shining example of faithfulness, service, and charity to those around her.[11] When she and John presided over the Guatemala Quetzaltenango

Carmen and John

Mission, they instituted a program to train missionaries in four Mayan languages so they could reach indigenous Guatemalans. Today there are over 280,000 Latter-day Saints in Guatemala's cities and the highlands, including Carmen's own family, who had initially opposed her marriage to John and her baptism into the Church.[12]

At the time of her passing at the age of seventy-five in 1998, Carmen had built a lasting legacy within her family (she had four children and twenty-six grandchildren) as well as within the Church. Throughout her life, Carmen thoughtfully considered local needs and offered suggestions to improve the lives of Latter-day Saints in Guatemala and Central America. She was an active participant in the Church and fearlessly used her voice for change. Her ideas and contributions influenced the way Latter-day Saints learn and worship throughout the world.[13]

When Carmen was in her late sixties, her husband, John, was called to be the president of the missionary training center in Peru. When they arrived at the MTC, however, they found the building to be insanitary. They requested and received approval from Church headquarters to oversee a complete renovation of the Peru MTC.

Chieko Nishimura Okazaki

1926–2011

Writer, Educator, and Religious Leader

"For by one Spirit are we all baptized into one body, whether we be Jews or Gentiles, whether we be bond or free; and have been all made to drink into one Spirit." 1 CORINTHIANS 12:13

BUILDING BRIDGES

Fifteen-year-old Chieko and her mom feverishly gathered all their Japanese possessions, including fans, books, and pictures, lit a big fire, and burned them. The Japanese military had just bombed Pearl Harbor, launching the United States into World War II. Citizens were in a state of unrest and fear. Chieko's parents were humble plantation laborers whose families had immigrated from Japan to the Hawaiian Islands. But now the United States was at war with the land of Chieko's heritage, and her family was frightened about what this conflict would mean for Japanese Americans. When the smoke died from their fire, Chieko looked in the mirror. "My eyes, my skin, and my hair are Japanese," she thought. "I will always be Japanese."[1]

The months and years following the onset of World War II were difficult for Chieko, but she wasn't left comfortless. She found solace in her testimony of Jesus Christ. She had been introduced to the gospel four years before the war began. A sister missionary had visited Chieko's junior high school and invited the students to attend a special religion class taught at the little chapel near the school.

Though Buddhist, Chieko and three other Japanese girls accepted the invitation. Attending that class was the beginning of Chieko's introduction to Christianity.[2] Buddhism had already taught Chieko to show "respect, love, and charity" toward others. These same principles, found within the gospel of Jesus Christ, built upon her beliefs, and resonated deeply within her. After four years of living as "both a Buddhist and a Mormon," Chieko was baptized a member of The Church of Jesus Christ of Latter-day Saints a few months after the bombing of Pearl Harbor.[3]

Chieko's decision to join the Church changed her life. She felt an added measure of peace, joy, and hope, which was needed more than ever during the war. Over the next several years, Japanese Americans were persecuted, sometimes violently. Driven by xenophobic fear, neighbors and others in the community questioned whether she and her family were spies or traitors. The US government even issued an order to incarcerate those of Japanese descent, including US citizens, in isolated concentration camps. Chieko's uncle was sent to one of these camps. Chieko was confused and scared. As a Japanese American, she realized things might happen to her and her family over which they'd have little control. But no matter what happened, she knew she needed to accept both parts of herself. She believed that doing so would help her be more accepting of her identity. She explained, "My Japaneseness is something I consecrate to the Lord along with other talents, abilities, and desires."[4]

After this realization, much of Chieko's life was dedicated to promoting understanding about *all*

> Chieko paid for her education by working as a maid, and her family lovingly sacrificed to help with her tuition. Her parents and two little brothers helped earn her tuition by making sandals out of tree leaves. They sold each pair of sandals for fifty cents.

facets of people's identities—including race, culture, language, and even trauma. She wanted to help people embrace differences and build bridges of understanding.

DIVERSITY IS A STRENGTH

Chieko sought to build bridges between cultures and races in both her professional career and in her Church callings. In the early 1950s, Chieko and her husband moved to Salt Lake City, Utah, where Chieko took a job as a second-grade teacher. After World War II, anti-Japanese sentiment ran high throughout the United States. Three mothers refused to allow their children to be in Chieko's class because she was Japanese.

Chieko with her husband, Edward, and sons, Kenneth and Robert

With radiance and poise, Chieko showed up on the first day of school wearing a fuchsia-colored dress and a flower tucked behind her ear. She greeted each child warmly as the mothers stood nearby. Soon, Chieko had won everyone over, and the three mothers requested that their children be transferred back into Chieko's class. The principal told them, "Opportunity only knocks once."[5]

One of Chieko's biggest opportunities to build bridges within the Church came when she was appointed to the Young Women general board. This appointment made her the first person of color to serve on any of the Church's general auxiliary boards. Chieko said she felt that she represented people of color from all over the world in that assignment.[6] "We need our differences," she explained. "Diversity is important to us as individuals and as a Church. Diversity is a strength, not a division."[7] She taught that it's okay if you're not exactly like the woman sitting next to you at church.

Chieko also had great concern for how those who had chosen to slip out of Church activity were sometimes treated. Teaching that they should be shown an increased amount of understanding rather than judgement, she believed individuals responded well when treated with respect and acceptance.[8]

Chieko was dedicated to fostering unity despite language barriers. After she was called to serve in the Relief Society General Presidency in 1990, President Gordon B. Hinckley gave her a blessing that her tongue might be loosed. Chieko didn't speak Spanish, Korean, or Tongan, but she had a great desire to deliver her talks in those languages when she traveled to lands where they were spoken. By speaking in her listeners' language, Chieko felt as if she was confirming that who they were was important and that they were just as valuable as the majority in the Church, who spoke English. Chieko enlisted the Church's translation department to translate her talks into Spanish, Korean, and Tongan. And then, with the help of others and by drawing strength from President Hinckley's blessing, Chieko fervently practiced her delivery. She would affectionately greet her audience with "Aloha" and then proceed to give her talk in her listeners' native language. Through this important and empathetic gesture, Chieko showed that

While attending the University of Hawaii, Chieko met Edward Okazaki, a decorated World War II veteran who had been part of the 442nd Infantry Regiment. They were married in 1949, and ten months later, Edward was baptized. They had two sons, Kenneth and Robert, who Chieko described as "strong and gentle and loving."

true disciples of Christ do not need to assimilate into a different culture to live a gospel-centered life. Of these experiences, Chieko said: "I could feel the Spirit carrying my words to their hearts, and I could feel 'the fruit of the Spirit' bringing back to me their love, their joy, and their faith. I could feel the Spirit making us one."[9]

No matter where she was in the world, Chieko powerfully shared her testimony of the Savior when addressing a congregation. She also didn't shy away from discussing difficult subjects. She opened the floodgates for the Church to address abuse in her landmark talk, "Healing from Sexual Abuse." In this talk, she confirmed that being abused is not the victim's fault, encouraged survivors to seek help, counseled listeners on how they could help those who had been abused, and testified of the love and empathy of God and Jesus Christ.[10]

Chieko and her husband were responsible for the Mormon Pavilion at the 1970 World's Fair in Osaka, Japan. Nearly seven million people visited their display. As a result, approximately 780,000 Japanese people requested for missionaries to visit them in their homes.

EMBRACING THE FUTURE WITH FAITH

Chieko was a remarkable woman. She grew up in poverty, converted to a new religion, struggled and sacrificed to gain an education, felt the sting of racial prejudice, learned to balance a family and career (she was a schoolteacher and a principal), bore the emotional and physical burdens of ill health (she was a triple breast cancer survivor), and struggled with the sudden loss of her beloved husband. She was a widow for twenty years until her death in 2011, at the age of eighty-four. Through it all, Chieko listened to the Spirit and touched many people's hearts through her words and ministry. And she kept the vow she made as a young girl—to continually build bridges of understanding by helping others to embrace diversity.[11]

Elsie Sreenivasam Dharmaraju

1929–2015

Trailblazer Who Took the Gospel to India

"And if it so be that you should labor all your days in crying repentance unto this people, and bring, save it be one soul unto me, how great shall be your joy with him in the kingdom of my Father!" **DOCTRINE AND COVENANTS 18:15**

A DYING FRIEND'S REQUEST

Elsie was moving away from her small town in India. But this move wasn't merely across town, across the country, or even across the continent. She was moving across the world to Samoa, an island country over seven thousand miles away from the land, customs, and people that were familiar to her. Elsie's husband, Edwin, was a renowned entomologist and had accepted a new job, which necessitated the long journey to Samoa. Although this area of the world was new to the couple, it didn't take long for them to make friends. Soon after their arrival, they befriended Lillian and Richard Ashby, an American couple living in Western Samoa. Richard was a doctor, and the Ashbys were serving a unique medical mission in a hospital in Apia.[1]

Lillian and Richard were members of The Church of Jesus Christ of Latter-day Saints and did their best to share the gospel with Elsie and Edwin. Initially, Elsie wasn't interested in the Church. She was the daughter of a devout Baptist minister, and Edwin's family had been loyal Anglicans for over a century. Everything changed, however, when Lillian learned that her breast cancer had returned. Prior to the Ashbys' mission call, Lillian's cancer had gone into remission after she received treatment. But when malignant cells reemerged, Lillian's health declined rapidly. Acknowledging the possibility of death, Lillian wrote her testimony in her white leatherbound Book of Mormon and made her husband promise that he'd give the book to Elsie and Edwin if she died. True to his word, when Lillian passed away in 1976, Richard delivered her scriptures to the Dharmarajus.[2]

Like most people in India, Elsie's family followed the tradition of arranged marriages, where parents choose their children's spouses. When Elsie's father asked her to meet Edwin Dharmaraju, a young man in their village whom he felt would make a good husband, Elsie trusted her father's judgment, and agreed. She and Edwin were married in 1950. Elsie said they "learned to love each other a great deal."

Elsie opened the Book of Mormon and read Lillian's touching testimony. Lillian's words, as well as the influence of the missionaries and Samoan Church members, prompted Elsie and Edwin to earnestly study the Book of Mormon and principles of the gospel. Within three months, Elsie and her family were baptized. Little did Elsie know that she would soon be instrumental in bringing The Church of Jesus Christ of Latter-day Saints to her homeland.[3]

AN INSTRUMENT IN HIS HANDS

Elsie and Edwin took every opportunity to share their conversion with others. When they traveled to India for their daughter's wedding, they enthusiastically discussed the restored gospel with their extended family. When they returned back home to Samoa, they wrote to Church headquarters and requested that missionaries be sent to India. Church leaders listened and responded with a special mission call—for Elsie and Edwin to return to India and teach their relatives for three months. The couple didn't want to go to India emptyhanded, so in preparation for their mission, they shipped nearly five hundred pounds of Church materials to India—all donated by fellow Latter-day Saints in Samoa.[4]

Just two months after the Dharmarajus started their mission, many in their extended family embraced the gospel. In December of 1978, they gathered around Elsie's brother-in-law's swimming pool, which had been cleaned, painted, and filled with fresh water. Twenty-two family members, including Edwin's parents, were baptized, and the first branch in India was organized in Hyderabad, Telangana.

Lillian's scriptures, in which she wrote her testimony for Elsie

Elsie knew that to further the missionary work in India, it was important for the Book of Mormon to be translated into Telugu, one of India's most widely spoken languages. And she had the perfect person in mind to do it: her father, Reverend P. Sreenivasam. Although the reverend hadn't joined the Church, he felt that the Book of Mormon was of great value. He was eighty-two years old and in poor health, but he began translating one page per day. Two years later, Elsie and Edwin delivered the seven-hundred-page manuscript to the prophet, Spencer W. Kimball. As a result of

The Dharmaraju family on the day they were baptized

Elsie and Edwin Dharmaraju (center) and their family before leaving American Samoa to serve their mission in India

their dedication and the gracious diligence of Elsie's father, selections of the Book of Mormon were made available in Telugu.[5]

EMBRACING THE FUTURE WITH FAITH

For the rest of their lives, Elsie and Edwin were committed to the Church and continued to share the gospel with zeal. When Edwin died, Elsie moved to the United States where she worked at the University of Utah and served as a Relief Society teacher in her ward. Even after she had been a widow for thirty years, she often visited her son and relatives in India, where she'd drop by the branch that she and her husband had helped organize.[6]

Prior to Elsie and Edwin's mission, The Church of Jesus Christ of Latter-day Saints had attempted to establish a presence in India for 125 years. Their efforts had been more or less unsuccessful until the Dharmarajus assumed the mantle of missionary work. The Church's presence continues to increase in India; in 2012, the first stake was organized in Hyderabad, and total Church membership has since surpassed fourteen thousand.[7] The Church continues to grow slowly but surely in India. Such growth didn't begin with the traditional missionary programs the Church implemented in other countries.

The Bengaluru Temple was announced in 2018, and construction for this historic temple, the first in India, began in December of 2020.

Rather, it began with the friendship between two women, a testimony written in a leatherbound Book of Mormon, and a Latter-day Saint's willingness to listen to the Spirit and share her love for the gospel with her family.[8]

While living in the Gilbert Islands, Elsie was a science teacher, and she later worked as a research assistant for the Department of Pharmacology and Toxicology at the University of Utah. All five of her children married and became scientists with graduate degrees.

Beverly Brough Campbell

1931–2017

Entrepreneur and Director of International Affairs for the Church

"Make you perfect in every good work to do his will, working in you that which is wellpleasing in his sight, through Jesus Christ." HEBREWS 13:21

IF YOU THINK IT

With a loving husband and new baby, Beverly had only ever thought about being a wife and mother. At the time, in the mid-1950s, it was common for fathers to be the sole breadwinners of the family, and many mothers were able to stay and raise their children at home. But when doctors thought Beverly's husband, Pierce, might have brain cancer, she realized her life might turn out differently than what she had anticipated. Beverly knew she'd have to make significant changes when Pierce's doctor pulled her aside and said, "You probably should be prepared to earn a living for the rest of your life."[1] This was a difficult time for Beverly, yet looking back, she realized everything that happened was preparing her for the future.

Fortunately, Pierce didn't have cancer—he had hypoglycemia. But this condition came with its own health challenges, which changed Pierce's career path and dramatically altered both his and Beverly's lives. Despite the difficulties, Beverly was

> Colleagues of Beverly said, "Don't ask Beverly Campbell to do it if you don't want it done."

determined to take action to support her loved ones. She thought, "What strengths do I have that can help my family?"[2] She had skills teaching, lecturing, and broadcasting on the radio. Drawing on those talents, she took a job teaching at finishing schools in the evenings and worked at an insurance company during the day. Beverly continued to take initiative, and it wasn't long before she realized she could develop a finishing school curriculum with more depth and less superficiality. Equipped with her parents' counsel "If you think it, you can do it," Beverly went on to open Classique, a chain of finishing schools she and Pierce managed together. The schools became so successful in the mid-fifties that they were highly recommended by the fashion magazines *Vogue* and *Glamour*.[3]

Beverly helped create the name "Special Olympics" and implement their first logo. The Special Olympics has become the world's largest sports organization for children and adults with special needs. They have partners in 172 countries and host events involving five million participants worldwide.

With Beverly's newfound business and networking experience, along with her natural poise and speaking abilities, she was able to make a name for herself. She and Pierce sold Classique and moved to Washington, DC, where she was eventually appointed as the director of the Joseph P. Kennedy Jr. Foundation and helped create the Special Olympics. She quickly established a reputation for being hardworking and intelligent.

Because of her experience with the media and her willingness to fearlessly stand up for what she believed in, Church leaders asked her to be their spokesperson on the Equal Rights Amendment in Virginia. This led to an appearance with the Relief Society General President, Barbara Smith, on a popular talk show, *Donahue*, to discuss the beliefs of many Latter-day Saint women. Beverly didn't want to appear on the show but said: "I had made covenants with the Lord that I would help at anytime and anywhere I was needed; . . . so with great trepidation, I said yes."[4] While on *Donahue*, Beverly and Barbara Smith spoke confidently about wanting equality for women. After her appearance on *Donahue*, the Church asked Beverly to serve as an official spokesperson on national issues.

Beverly, President George H. W. Bush, and Elder M. Russell Ballard

Within a few years, Beverly was asked to be the Church's regional public affairs director for the northeast area of the United States. This assignment allowed her to develop lasting relationships with people from around the world, which proved to be invaluable when she was appointed to be the director of international affairs for the Church—her most important role yet.[5]

OPENING DOORS

When international problems arose for the Church, Latter-day Saint leaders called upon Beverly for help. With ingenuity, she found the right resources and people to solve them. Beverly's skills were put to the test in the early 1980s. At that time, Church leaders had few ties with foreign ambassadors and other government leaders, but Beverly knew how important these connections were for gaining access to the two-thirds of the world's nations in which the Church wasn't recognized. To provide places for foreign officials and Church leaders to mingle, Beverly invited foreign diplomats and ambassadors individually to dinners at her home in Virginia. There,

Beverly, President Russell M. Nelson, and the Vice Premier of China, Li Lanqinq, in Beijing, 1995

these international dignitaries met well-known Latter-day Saint leaders, politicians, and businesspeople. These important dinners provided an informal setting in which people could talk freely, build friendships, earn trust, and learn more about one another.

Because of her large network of connections, Beverly was able to arrange a meeting at her home between Elder Russell M. Nelson of the Quorum of the Twelve Apostles and Miroslav Houstecky, the Czechoslovak Soviet Socialist Republic's ambassador. After dinner, the two men retreated to her study. Elder Nelson presented the Church's desire to practice openly in Czechoslovakia. Houstecky listened and arranged a meeting that led to the granting of legal authority for Latter-day Saints to practice their religion. After forty years, the Church was finally recognized in Czechoslovakia.[6] Elder Nelson said, "Beverly was instrumental in establishing contact for me with the government leaders from Hungary, Poland, Czechoslovakia, and Russia."[7]

EMBRACING THE FUTURE WITH FAITH

Before Beverly became the director of international affairs, Church leaders had already tried to make connections with foreign government officials, but these efforts were met with little or no success.[8] But with Beverly's singular ability to facilitate meaningful connections between people, the Church gained recognition in thirty-nine countries, as well as new access to many more during her twelve-year tenure as director. During her time in that position, new missions were established in eight Eastern European countries, including Bulgaria, Ukraine, and Czechoslovakia. The Church still uses Beverly's methods of establishing personal friendships with ambassadors and other government officials today. President M. Russell Ballard of the Quorum of the Twelve Apostles said, "The Church of Jesus Christ of Latter-day Saints came out of the darkness because of the great work of this good woman."[9]

These successes are only a fraction of the accomplishments Beverly achieved through her initiative, talents, and willingness to serve. Throughout her life, she fine-tuned her natural talents and fostered new ones to become a powerful leader, a dynamic spokesperson, and a faithful servant of the Lord. She authored landmark books, including *Eve and the Choice Made in Eden*.[10] As a speaker and author, she was a role model for countless girls and women, reminding them of their divine identity as well as the importance of relying on Heavenly Father.

> In memory of her daughter, Heather Ann, who was killed in a car accident at the age of twenty-three, Beverly and her family established a foundation which drilled wells, built dams, and provided textbooks for children in Zimbabwe.

As a young mother, Beverly had intended to create a safe and spiritual home for her family. She not only achieved this with her husband and three children but she also opened doors throughout the world so other families could experience the light of the gospel. Through her words and example, she also empowered all women—the wife and mother, the working woman, the teenager in Young Women—to stand up for what they believed in. President Russell M. Nelson said Beverly was a "wonderful wife, marvelous mother, devoted disciple of the Lord, and an angelic example to all. [She] fulfilled every assignment and served with dignity, courage, and wisdom."[11]

Wynetta Willis
Martin Clark

1938–2000

Singer Who Made History in the Tabernacle Choir

"For my soul delighteth in the song of the heart; yea, the song of the righteous is a prayer unto me, and it shall be answered with a blessing upon their heads." **DOCTRINE AND COVENANTS 25:12**

A CHURCH TOURIST

Even as a child, Wynetta felt like something was missing from her life—something as important as the very air she breathed. That something was a God whom she loved and trusted, a God who loved His children and was intimately aware of their hopes and feelings. Although Wynetta's parents read from the Bible and attended church, the God that Wynetta learned about was frightening and cruel. At a young age, she determined that if this portrayal of God reflected His true nature, she couldn't possibly love Him.[1] Wynetta didn't find peace in religion, but she did find that music helped her express everything in her heart and mind. Lyrics and melodies became a way for her to offer prayer.[2]

Even in her twenties, Wynetta struggled to connect with any specific religion. She described herself as a "tourist" because she visited one church after another, never staying at one for long.[3] She tried to discover truth in these churches, but she still felt emptiness and believed the thing that was missing from her life would

Of her membership in The Church of Jesus Christ of Latter-day Saints, Wynetta said: "This is my life and this is my peace."

remain missing forever. But one night, Wynetta had a profound experience that nurtured her faith in a loving God. As she was lying in her bed, a terrible darkness overcame her. Her mouth felt dry, her head and stomach ached with pain, and a roaring filled her ears. An indescribable power caused her to feel helpless and horrified, and in her desperation, Wynetta uttered the most heartfelt prayer of her life: "Dear God. . . . Please, please help me now in my most desperate hour of need." All of a sudden, a feeling of peace permeated Wynetta's soul. She thought she felt a soothing touch on her brow, and she heard a voice speak gently: "Be still, and know that I am God." Feeling awestruck and grateful, Wynetta finally found the God she had hoped for ever since she was a little girl. She knew that He was real and that He was kind. The only thing left to do was to find a religion that shared her testimony of Him.[4]

A MARVELOUS VOICE

Wynetta stumbled upon such a religion in the unlikeliest of ways. Following a minor surgery on her leg, Wynetta had to recover in a post-op unit. At first, she felt nervous; she worried the patient who shared her room would object to her skin color. Wynetta's roommate was named Barbara Weston. Not only did Barbara appear to be without racial prejudice, but she was also funny, bubbly, friendly, and talkative. Wynetta felt there was something unique about Barbara. Her new friend emanated a light that was warm, loving, and comforting. Barbara was a member of The Church of Jesus Christ of Latter-day Saints and spoke briefly about her beliefs. Intrigued, Wynetta asked Barbara to tell her more about her church, and for the next five days, they talked about this religion endlessly. They even avoided taking their sleeping pills so they could continue their

discussions late into the night. Wynetta felt truly converted to the gospel when she read the account of
Joseph Smith. As she read about his experience with
the adversary in the Sacred Grove, she immediately
thought of her own harrowing experience with the
suffocating darkness. Two months after leaving the

> Wynetta was well
> loved her whole
> life. Her jokester
> personality drew
> others to her.

hospital, Wynetta was baptized and learned more about the God
she had been searching for since her childhood.[5]

When Wynetta became a member of the Church, she aspired
to join the Tabernacle Choir. Music was such an important part of
her life, and she already had experience with live performances.
When she was a teenager, she sang in the Willis & Johnson Quartette

Wynetta (left) and Marilyn Yuille Norris,
who were the first Black members of the Tabernacle Choir

and performed dozens of times in the Los Angeles area.[6] Wynetta decided to take the plunge, and she prepared to audition for the Tabernacle Choir. She obtained recommendations from both her bishop and stake president, but she had difficulty scheduling an audition with Brother Richard Condie, the conductor of the choir. Months

> Throughout her life, Wynetta was described as "an exuberant and happy member of the Church."

passed before Wynetta was able to audition for the choir, but when the time finally came, she was terribly nervous. During the audition, Brother Condie smiled at her warmly and genuinely, which helped her relax. After forty-five minutes of vocal exercises, Brother Condie said: "Well, you made it. . . . I hope you thank God very often for your marvelous voice." Wynetta was stunned. Her hands trembled as Brother Condie shook her hand, and the realization sank in: she was a member of the Tabernacle Choir.[7]

EMBRACING THE FUTURE WITH FAITH

When Wynetta was a child, she frequently dreamed of being a missionary, of serving and lifting others' burdens.[8] Little did she know that she would fulfill this dream by singing in one of the world's largest and most famous choirs. Wynetta and another young woman named Marilyn Yuille Norris were the first Black members of the Tabernacle Choir. The choir toured throughout the country, and Wynetta was awestruck by the opportunity to sing for the president of the United States in Washington, DC. She toured the White House, visited many historical sites, and even got to see the president turn on the lights of the Christmas tree in Washington Square Park. Wynetta said it was "[her] dream come true."[9]

Wynetta was invited to participate in many singing and speaking engagements. She shared her story in hundreds of sacrament meetings, firesides, and seminary classes with the goal of bringing people to Christ and eradicating prejudices in the Church. She shared how the gospel had guided her to the missing piece of her life that she had yearned for as a child. It gave her a newfound purpose, which helped her discover her self-worth, and it prompted her to have more compassion.[10] The gospel helped her realize a dream, in which she sang alongside 359 other members of the Tabernacle Choir. She wrote, "As I sing, I sing with all parts of myself to show the great gladness I feel for my life."[11]

Becky
Douglas

1952–PRESENT

Founder of Organization That Helps People with Hansen's Disease

"Now ye may suppose that this is foolishness in me; but behold I say unto you, that by small and simple things are great things brought to pass." ALMA 37:6

THE SUFFERING OF ONE

When a psychiatrist diagnosed Amber with bipolar disorder, Becky knew next to nothing about the illness that afflicted her eldest daughter. She just knew that Amber was suffering, and Becky was desperate to help her. The psychiatrist tried to explain the symptoms that often accompany bipolar disorder—the severe shifts in mood and impairment of daily functioning. When the psychiatrist told Becky to prepare for the worst, she was simultaneously filled with disbelief, fear, and a fierce determination to get Amber through this challenge.

Becky and her husband, John, prayed constantly. They fasted for their daughter each week, attended the temple, and worked with a team of mental health professionals to help Amber. They did this for nearly eight years, but Amber grew worse. She attempted suicide multiple times and spent months in a mental health hospital. Every suicide attempt filled Becky with fear. She promised Heavenly Father that she'd sacrifice anything if He'd lift Amber's burden.[1]

But in 2000, Amber passed away by suicide while at college. Upon hearing the tragic news, Becky thought she would die. Her grief was so overwhelming, so agonizing that she wondered if she could move forward from this loss. One day, as Becky sorted through her daughter's belongings, she discovered that Amber had been donating some of her money to an orphanage in India. When the Douglas family held Amber's funeral, they asked that people donate money to that same orphanage in lieu of giving flowers. The generosity of well-wishers stunned Becky. The sum of the donations was so substantial that the orphanage asked Becky to be a member of the board. Intrigued by the offer, Becky decided to travel to India to learn more about the country, the culture, and the orphanage.

After Becky had seven biological children, she adopted three more—two children from Lithuania and one child from India.

"YOU ARE SOMEONE"

Becky visited the orphanage and observed the needs of the children who lived there. But the most unforgettable part of the trip was not her visit to the orphanage. It was driving through the streets of Chennai, where she saw many beggars. The physical suffering of these people was unlike anything Becky had ever seen. Many of the beggars had big, gaping wounds that oozed with pus and blood. Their hands and feet were rotting and severely deformed. Some of the beggars didn't have eyes. One man reached his hand out toward Becky, and she saw maggots crawling through his mangled flesh. The sight was ghastly, and the stench of decay was oppressive. Becky asked in disbelief, "Who are these people?" The driver said, "Oh, those are the lepers"—the "untouch-ables"—who were believed to be cursed and defiled. Becky almost didn't believe him. She thought Hansen's disease, formerly known as leprosy, was a thing of the past, a vicious disease that existed only in biblical times. But here it was, afflicting the very people who were press-ing themselves against the car, begging her for money. Becky looked away, appalled and heartbroken by their suffering.

Rising Star Outreach provides an education from kindergarten to twelfth grade for children from the colonies.

The memory of the beggars seared itself in Becky's mind, and that night, in her hotel room, she prayed. She asked, "What can I do? I'm just a mom, a housewife!" She felt surprised when a small suggestion came to mind: Look at them. Acknowledge the suffering of these people. The following day, Becky committed to looking at the people with Hansen's disease. She wanted to be like the Savior, whose interactions with the afflicted were suffused with love and kindness. But when Becky set her eyes upon the beggars' deformi-ties, and the stench of human decomposition filled her nostrils, she wanted to get away as soon as possible. At a stoplight, one woman crawled to the car, her belly chafing against the sweltering street. She tried to get the passengers' attention by scratching at the car's tires. The driver instructed Becky to lean her head out the window and tell the woman to move, so she wouldn't get run over when the stoplight turned green. Becky opened the window and motioned for the woman to get away from the car. But then they locked eyes, and Becky saw a mother gazing back at her—a woman and a human being, just like her.

Becky and children at the entrance of the Amber Douglas Home for Girls

That interaction haunted Becky for several days, and she thought someone should do something for the people with Hansen's disease. After returning home, on one particularly sleepless night, Becky woke up and thought, "*You* are someone. Do something." She called four of her friends, and together, they met around Becky's kitchen table and formed Rising Star Outreach, a charity dedicated to serving those with Hansen's disease in India. When her husband came home from work that night, Becky excitedly told him about the new organization. John was taken aback and asked her what she knew about India, Hansen's disease, medicine, or running a business. He asked her what she was going to do. Undeterred, Becky responded, "I don't know, but I'm going to do something."

EMBRACING THE FUTURE WITH FAITH

Rising Star Outreach has grown substantially since its start in 2001. But at its conception, Becky had to learn through trial and error how to create an organization that would have a sustainable impact on the settlements, known as the "leprosy colonies," where people with Hansen's disease were isolated. At first, she brought rice and beans to the colonies but soon realized that if she fed the people that day, then she'd have to return and feed them the next day, and the next day. Rising Star Outreach tried to provide economic rehabilitation and medical care: it started some small businesses for people in the colonies, and volunteers attempted to treat people's leprous wounds. But the businesses ended up failing, and continuously cutting out rotten flesh wasn't the most effective way to treat the disease.

Things changed, however, with the help of donations, volunteers, key partnerships, and collaborations. Rising Star Outreach helped people with Hansen's disease obtain microloans so they could begin their own businesses. When people paid back the loans, the money was then offered to another family that wanted to start a business. The microloans resulted in the creation of over one hundred businesses, including a tea business, a beauty parlor, a barbershop, a trucking business, a sari shop, and an auto-transportation business. These endeavors succeeded because the people with Hansen's disease started the businesses themselves; they have an intimate knowledge of the needs of their community, and they feel a sense of pride and ownership over their endeavors.

Becky has completed more than sixty trips to India! Rising Star Outreach has to renew its charity license every five years to continue its work in the colonies.

For medical services, the organization partnered with a doctor who joined the board and helped them establish their first mobile medical unit. These units provide medical care, screenings, and wound self-care programs for those with Hansen's disease. The organization has offered tens of thousands of treatments, including multidrug therapy, a combination of antibiotics that can cure the disease. Rising

Rising Star Outreach believes educating children from the colonies is one of the best ways to fight the stigma associated with Hansen's disease.

Star Outreach also created schools to educate children who live in the colonies and has produced more than 160 high school graduates. Some of these graduates are now college-bound or are already enrolled in college.[2]

Among these many successes, one of Rising Star Outreach's most meaningful accomplishments was the creation of a boarding school for children from leprosy colonies. The J. Willard and Alice S. Marriott Foundation paid for the school and named the girls' dormitory "The Amber Douglas Home for Girls." Whenever Becky walks into the dormitory and sees Amber's picture, she feels the Spirit. She's filled with joy whenever a little girl approaches her and says, "Auntie, I live in 'the Amber.'" Amber's death was the worst experience of Becky's life, but it led her to create a charitable organization that has changed countless lives, including Becky's.

One of the most profound lessons Becky has learned is that a seemingly inconsequential act of love from one individual can have an extraordinary influence on a family, a community, and even an entire country. Continuing to serve in India is challenging because it's difficult for Rising Star Outreach to renew their foreign funding license. The Foreign Contribution Regulation Act (FCRA) has already rejected thousands of applications from other charities, making the future of Rising Star Outreach uncertain. But Becky relies on the grace of God and believes He will continue to send miracles. She knows because she's witnessed countless miracles already, many of which stemmed from the miracle of Amber's small donations and God's ability to bring beauty from tragedy.

Emelia Mould
Ahadjie

1962–PRESENT

Church Employee Who Stood Firm during Military Opposition

"Be of good courage, and he shall strengthen your heart, all ye that hope in the Lord." PSALM 31:24

A GAME OF HIDE-AND-SEEK

Emelia was a bright, curious, and hardworking woman who sought after knowledge and enjoyed learning new things. But when her cousin exclaimed, "Emelia, I have found a new church. . . . It's The Church of Jesus Christ of Latter-day Saints!" she didn't match his enthusiasm. Rather, she merely replied, "I'm really not interested in any church." It wasn't that Emelia didn't believe in God. On the contrary, she and her family were Christian, and they found solace in God during difficult times. However, Emelia had had some bad experiences with other denominations. Promises were broken, expectations were dashed, and she'd had enough. Her cousin didn't give up so easily; he assured Emelia that the Church members were good people, and he begged her to meet with the missionaries. Emelia tried to make herself scarce. When she saw the missionaries coming, she hid and instructed her cousin to tell them that she

Like Nephi, Emelia says she was "born of goodly parents." Her parents taught her to "brighten the corner" wherever she is through service, faith, and hard work.

was unavailable. Although Emelia became adept at dodging the missionaries, she wondered if she should meet with the elders once, just to please her cousin. After all, she had moved from Nsawam to Accra, Ghana, to find work, and her cousin had been graciously allowing her to stay with him. She wanted it to stay that way!

After several invitations and pleas from her cousin, Emelia allowed the missionaries to begin teaching her. Emelia wondered what the missionaries could possibly teach her since she already knew the scriptures so well. But to appease her cousin, Emelia said yes to every one of the missionaries' requests. She said yes when they asked if she'd complete assignments. She said yes when they wanted to schedule follow-up lessons. She even said yes when they asked if she'd be baptized. On the day of her baptism, Emelia seemed to vanish into thin air. Even though she ran away on her own baptism day, the missionaries still wanted to teach her.

The missionaries' passion for the gospel piqued Emelia's curiosity. She decided to learn more about their faith, and she began to ask them questions. They invited her to a missionary fireside where she watched *The Windows of Heaven,* a film about the law of tithing. Emelia got the chills as she watched the movie, but the crowning jewel of her investigation was when she learned about the plan of salvation. She marveled that the Church clearly spelled out the plan of salvation: "They made me understand my purpose on earth— that I'm not here by chance but that my life has a meaning and a purpose." Soon, Emelia entreated the missionaries to tell her more about the gospel, and this time she genuinely desired to be baptized. On a joyous Tuesday evening, Emelia was baptized as a member of The Church of Jesus Christ of Latter-day Saints. Once Emelia joined the Church, she was put to work immediately. She was called to serve as the second counselor in the Primary presidency the day after her baptism, and a month later, she was called as the Young Women president. But Emelia didn't stop there. In December of 1988, she began her employment for the Church and worked as the mission secretary in Accra.

THE FREEZE

Emelia had not been a member for long, but her faith was tested in ways she couldn't possibly have imagined. On June 14, 1989, Emelia and her colleagues heard an alarming announcement. The government had banned all church meetings for The Church of Jesus Christ of Latter-day Saints and Jehovah's Witnesses. Some leaders in Ghana perceived the presence of these religious groups as a threat.[1] As a result, meetinghouses were locked, some members were imprisoned, and missionaries were deported and forbidden from entering Ghana.

The situation was both frightening and disorienting. A group of armed soldiers ordered everyone to leave the mission home. Everyone left— except for Emelia. As she hid in the mission office, she thought of Esther,

In December 2019, Emelia (forefront) received the Long Service Award for over thirty years of service as an employee for The Church of Jesus Christ of Latter-day Saints.

who was willing to sacrifice herself to save her people from destruction.[2] Emelia thought she heard a voice of an angel, telling her that

Emelia's Church employment was the direct result of a testimony she bore in sacrament meeting. When the missionaries heard her testimony, they got formal approval to hire her, so she could start working immediately.

she was a strong woman. If the military killed her, she thought, then so be it. The military eventually kicked the door open and found Emelia in the mission office. They were dumbfounded by her stubbornness and demanded to know why she hadn't left the compound. With poise and courage, Emelia simply responded, "I'm here because of you." Emelia knew the military had to communicate with Church leaders in Salt Lake City, and she told them that she was the only remaining person who knew how to use the telex machine, a communication device with a typewriter-like keyboard. The military realized that she was right and that they needed her help. Because of the time difference in Utah, Emelia had to sleep in the office for many months—away from the comforts of her own home and away from her husband on weekdays—so she could keep lines of communication open between the Ghanaian government and Church leaders.

"The Freeze" continued for eighteen months, but this did not deter many faithful members in Ghana. Some Latter-day Saints met in the forest to worship, and they'd travel for miles in order to minister to each family. After the Church was cleared of its accusations and the ban was lifted, some members didn't return to church, but others returned to their meetinghouses with joy and gratitude. Because they had been subjected to the refiner's fire, the Saints' faith had been bolstered, and their testimonies burned brighter than ever.

EMBRACING THE FUTURE WITH FAITH

Where did that leave Emelia? When the tension subsided after "the Freeze," she continued to work for the Church. She became the first executive secretary to the mission president. She organized conferences, served on the committee for a temple groundbreaking, and coordinated travel for missionaries, apostles, and even President Gordon B. Hinckley. She was the first female Church employee in West Africa and worked as the Africa West Area director of public affairs before retiring in January 2022. Emelia knows that life is full of challenges: "We were never promised that the journey will be easy, but by His grace and His love, all things will work together for good to those who believe in Him." Who knew that the stubbornness that once caused Emelia to flee from the missionaries was the very quality that allowed her to stand up to the military, defend her faith, and testify of God.

Sahar
Qumsiyeh

1971–PRESENT

Convert Who Found Peace amid Political Unrest

"If ye have faith as a grain of mustard seed, ye shall say unto this mountain, Remove hence to yonder place; and it shall remove; and nothing shall be impossible unto you." MATTHEW 17:20

NO NATIONALITY, NO HOME

Sahar was in the fifth grade when her teacher instructed her and the other frightened students to stay in the classroom for safety. It was dangerous to be outside. Close to the school, civilians were demonstrating against the Israeli occupation, and soldiers fired rubber bullets and tear gas to disperse the protesters. When one of the students opened the door to the classroom, an active tear gas bomb flew into the room. Chaos erupted, and Sahar's ears filled with the cries of her terror-stricken classmates. Fortunately, no one was hurt, but the incident intensified the students' alarm. When Sahar eventually left her school to return home, she had to walk past the soldiers. At the time, she didn't understand what was going on or why people were demonstrating; she just felt terrified of the soldiers and didn't want them to hurt her.

Sahar grew up in Beit Sahour, a town close to Bethlehem. She loved her little town, but it became harder and harder for her to feel peace and safety in the place she called home. Sahar is Palestinian, but her country and nationality no longer existed once the State of

Israel occupied the whole of the country in 1967.[1] Many Palestinians became refugees and were denied basic human rights and liberties, restricted from travel, and terrorized for protesting Israel's occupation.

Sahar (left) as a child with her friend Rana

As time passed, the situation only worsened. An uprising ensued, people were arrested or killed, checkpoints restricted travel for Palestinians, a curfew was established, and the number of demonstrations increased. Shootings, the sound of gunshots, beatings, tear gas, dehumanization—they all became a part of "normal" life. Sahar believed God existed, but the God she conceptualized was indifferent and perhaps even vengeful. With the violence and injustices perpetuated toward Palestinians, she thought that God hated her. She believed that if she were to pray, God wouldn't listen. Little did Sahar know that God was already guiding her; she just didn't realize it yet.

"I COULDN'T WALK AWAY"

When it came time for Sahar to attend graduate school, American University in Washington, DC, offered her a full scholarship. It was a generous offer, and Sahar intended to accept it and pursue a master's degree in statistics. But one day, she read her local paper and noticed an ad from a school called Brigham Young University. BYU was offering four scholarships specifically for Palestinians. Sahar decided to apply, even though she felt confident that she'd attend

American University. A few weeks later, the director of the BYU Jerusalem Center called Sahar to inform her that she had been awarded the scholarship. This scholarship was significantly less money than the scholarship from American University, but Sahar felt inexplicably drawn to BYU. Sahar's friends and family told her to choose American University, saying the choice was obvious. But Sahar kept having the unshakeable thought that she should attend BYU. Sahar didn't know why she should choose this school, nor did she understand that what she was feeling was actually a spiritual prompting. She just knew that she couldn't deny the power of the feeling, so she made up her mind, packed her belongings, and moved to Provo, Utah.[2]

At first, it wasn't easy being at BYU. Sahar struggled to feel a sense of belonging, especially since nobody seemed to be aware of what was happening in Palestine. She also thought the students' religion—that of The Church of Jesus Christ of Latter-day Saints—was flat-out strange. She heard stories about men with multiple wives and was bewildered to learn that members couldn't drink tea or coffee. But one day, Sahar watched general conference with her friends. She had heard that Latter-day Saints believed in a living prophet, and she

When the Israeli military closed Bethlehem University, college students met in secret to resume their studies. Sahar and her classmates met in the home of a student or a faculty member for class.

Sahar at the entrance of a checkpoint

was curious to learn more about it. During one session, something unbelievable happened: a speaker named Howard W. Hunter referred to her home country as "Palestine," not "Israel," which she heard so often.[3] Sahar felt like her identity was erased whenever someone referred to her home as Israel, but President Hunter correctly named her country. She thought, "They acknowledged my rights, so this must be a good church." Sahar asked her friend to tell her all about the Church. They talked about the Creation and the Fall, the Restoration of the gospel, the Godhead, and how Jesus Christ atoned for humankind's sins.

In 2007, Sahar earned a PhD in statistics and later got a job as a faculty member at BYU–Idaho.

Sahar continued to learn more about the Church with eagerness. A friend gave her a Book of Mormon in Arabic, and she read it cover to cover. She attended church and eventually wanted to get baptized. When Sahar called home with trepidation to tell her parents her news, they were angry. They told her that she'd be ostracized and that she was betraying the family. They believed the Latter-day Saints had brainwashed her and that she was making a huge mistake. Sahar felt torn because she didn't want to hurt her family, but she realized that she couldn't walk away from something so important to her. She made one of the most important decisions of her life and was baptized in 1996.

EMBRACING THE FUTURE WITH FAITH

Sahar knew that joining the Church was the best path for her, but nobody promised it would be an easy one. After graduate school, Sahar moved back home to Beit Sahour and faced the scorn of her family. They mocked her and tried to convince her to leave the Church. Sahar's mother threatened to burn her scriptures, and her family even refused to speak to her on the weekends she went to church. It was painful to see her family so upset with her, but Sahar remembered how miserable she felt prior to finding the gospel. The Church had helped her find joy and peace, and she never wanted to let go of the knowledge that she was a daughter of God.

Sahar found refuge when she attended church, but the journey to her branch in Jerusalem was difficult. Because of the travel restrictions and checkpoints the State of Israel had imposed, she had to climb hills, march through dusty dirt roads, take long detours, hide from soldiers, and even squeeze through a hole in a separation wall. Sometimes, her trip would take hours, and each week, it only got harder. For twelve years, Sahar risked her life to attend her branch.

Sahar in Jerusalem

Although she knew God would not want to put her in danger, she felt that He would protect her.

On one occasion, it was impossible to get to church because a curfew had been established; anybody found outside during curfew would be shot. Sahar wanted to go to church, but she didn't know how. All she could do was walk outside, so she did. There, on her small street, she saw a taxi. Not only was it unusual to see a taxi in such a secluded area, but it was also unheard of to see one during curfew. As it happened, this taxi was on its way to Jerusalem, so Sahar hitched a ride. The driver knew where all of the soldiers were stationed, and he avoided them by driving through hayfields and dirt roads. When they came to a road that was blocked by a large pile of rocks, he drove off the path and into a field where he zipped around olive trees. The driver's car was small and looked ready to fall apart at any moment, but they arrived safely in Jerusalem, and Sahar was able to attend church.

> Sahar wrote *Peace for a Palestinian*, a book that shares her story and search for peace. Deseret Book published her book in 2017.

Today Sahar is a professor at BYU–Idaho, and she doesn't need to climb through hilly landscapes or evade armed mercenaries to attend sacrament meeting. Now, she feels privileged to live just minutes away from a church building. But when she remembers that impossible taxi ride to the branch in Jerusalem, she knows that her success in attending church was an absolute miracle. She learned that when she does all that she can, even if it's taking just one step forward, God takes care of her. There have been many times in Sahar's life when she wanted to give up, but she's witnessed the growth of her faith as she's climbed the steepest mountains: "If you have faith as a grain of a mustard seed, you can move mountains

. . . but sometimes mountains aren't meant to be moved. Sometimes when those mountains don't move, we need the faith to climb them and not necessarily the faith to move them. Climbing those mountains is a path that will get us closer to God."

Mihaela Ganea King

1972–PRESENT

Mother Who Endured Infertility and Miscarriage

"I know that [God] loveth his children; nevertheless, I do not know the meaning of all things." **1 NEPHI 11:17**

WHEN LIFE DOESN'T GO AS PLANNED

"Getting pregnant should be easy," thought Mihaela, as she and her husband, Sterling, talked about starting a family. The Kings felt a greater sense of urgency than most newlyweds to have children right away. By the time they married, both Mihaela and Sterling were in their late thirties. Although the risks associated with childbirth increase with age, Mihaela wasn't too concerned. She assumed she'd be like her mom, who seemed able to bear children with ease. With excitement and confidence, the couple immediately started trying for a baby, but one year later, Mihaela still wasn't pregnant.

This wasn't Mihaela's first hardship. She grew up in Romania during a period of fear and oppression. When the Communists assumed power in Romania, they attempted to eradicate the country's cultural traditions and creative freedoms. The government demolished historical buildings, churches, and other architectural treasures. They denied the existence of God, and anybody found worshipping God or challenging the government's ideology could be imprisoned, tortured, or killed. It was at great risk that Mihaela's parents planned to flee the country. Their home was bugged, so they could only discuss their preparations at a park. If they were caught escaping Romania, they would be killed for committing treason. Despite the government's threats and intimidations, her family miraculously obtained passports and visas to leave the country.

This experience was one of the many ways Mihaela learned that God is powerful and that He helps those who "keep moving."

Mihaela has played the violin for over forty years. She studied violin at competitive conservatories and programs, and she's played for several professional orchestras.

Mihaela didn't give up on starting a family, even after a year of failed efforts to get pregnant. The Kings went to see a fertility specialist. They tried a variety of treatments for an entire year, but nothing worked. At that point, their doctor recommended IVF (in vitro fertilization). Although IVF can increase a woman's chance of becoming pregnant, it's expensive. One treatment can cost as much as $25,000, and there's no guarantee that the treatment will work. Upon discovering the cost of IVF, Mihaela's heart fell, and she wept. The Kings didn't have the funds, and their dream of having children seemed further away than ever. It pained Mihaela's mom to see her daughter's despair, so she decided to refinance her home to help the couple pay for treatments. Grateful for her mom's generosity, Mihaela started IVF with renewed hope. The very first treatment worked, and the Kings were overjoyed when Mihaela gave birth to their first child, Lincoln.

When Lincoln was nine months old, the couple tried IVF again, but it was unsuccessful. Even though IVF was costly and hard on her body and spirit, Mihaela wanted to give it a third try. Sterling, on the other hand, felt hesitant and thought they should be content with one child. They fasted and prayed for a year and sought priesthood blessings until one day they received spiritual confirmation to try again. They tried IVF for a third time and had an ultrasound at six weeks—there were two heartbeats! Mihaela and Sterling could barely contain their excitement, but at their eight-week ultrasound, one twin's heartbeat had disappeared. Saddened by their loss, Mihaela tried to focus on the remaining baby in her womb and prayed for its health. When she was ten weeks pregnant, her doctor said it was okay for her to tell friends and family. Then, at thirteen weeks, Mihaela had an appointment with her ob-gyn for another ultrasound. She reassured Sterling that she could attend the appointment on her own because the chance of miscarriage was low, and she felt confident that all would be well. When Mihaela had her ultrasound, however, there was no heartbeat. Her baby had died.

Mihaela herself almost died from the miscarriage; it was painful and dangerous, and she experienced excessive blood loss. She then sank into a deep depression and mourned the loss of her babies. She didn't understand why Heavenly Father would give her such a powerful confirmation to try IVF again when it would ultimately end in tragedy. She couldn't go to church for a few months because when people asked how she was doing, she would break down in tears.

After weeks of despair and grief, Mihaela woke up one Monday morning and felt . . . happy. It was like her depression had disappeared, and she was baffled. When she told Sterling, he said the bishopric had fasted and prayed for her the day before. Mihaela knew that the miracle had come from their fast, and she felt like her burden was lifted. Questions about her loss still occupied her mind, but she clung onto three things: God loved her, He cared about her, and He didn't want to hurt her.

Mihaela with her husband, Sterling, and children

"THERE'S ANOTHER BABY"

By the time Mihaela felt ready to try for another baby, she had a strong sense that IVF would no longer be a good option for her. She and Sterling explored other options to expand their family and learned about embryo donation. After prayerful consideration, the Kings determined this was the right option for their family. One embryo was successfully transferred to Mihaela's womb, and after a healthy pregnancy, the Kings were thrilled to welcome their second baby, Alden.[1]

Although Mihaela adored Lincoln and Alden with all her heart, she knew their family wasn't done growing yet. She had an unmistakable, spiritual impression that there was another baby. The Kings went to a fertility specialist and initially intended to transfer one embryo to Mihaela's womb. The embryo wasn't developing properly, but they didn't want to discard it, so they decided to keep it and transfer an additional embryo since the chance of an ill-developed embryo surviving was slim. But during an ultrasound, the Kings were surprised to discover not one, but two, distinct heartbeats.

EMBRACING THE FUTURE WITH FAITH

The pregnancy was hard on Mihaela, and she was on bedrest for the majority of her term. She went into labor at thirty-two weeks and had Abram, who was five pounds, and Caroline, who was three pounds. While the doctors were attending to Caroline, Abram stopped breathing for five minutes. The lack of oxygen resulted in brain damage, and Abram was diagnosed with cerebral palsy, a neurological disorder that affects his motor abilities. He requires constant care and has received many innovative treatments and therapies to help him progress. Every day is a challenge. Mihaela often feels overwhelmed because Abram is completely dependent on her, and yet she also has to attend to her other children's needs. Mihaela relies on Heavenly Father to sustain her each day. She admits the challenges of raising Abram, but she savors the joyous moments—like when he meets a milestone, says a new word, or greets her with a smile when he wakes up each morning.

As a younger woman, Mihaela had planned out her whole life. She thought she'd marry in her twenties and have children soon after. But after marrying at thirty-seven years old, struggling with infertility, undergoing painful IVF treatments, suffering a miscarriage, and raising a child with special needs, she's realized that life doesn't always go exactly as planned. But as she's reflected on the love she feels for her husband and children, she sees a beautiful, rich, and fulfilling life. Mihaela still doesn't understand why she lost her first twins or why Abram has cerebral palsy. As time passes, however, she thinks that perhaps the "why" doesn't matter. Perhaps there's something more she needs to focus on: "Looking back at my life, I feel like God has a plan for each of us, . . . and my job is to trust His plan." Mihaela acknowledges that when it feels like everything is going wrong, it's so easy to stop trying, to quit. But she's learned that God takes care of His children, and when we keep moving, even when it feels like there's no hope, we're in a much better position to receive help and guidance from our Heavenly Father.

> Abram blesses the King family immeasurably. Mihaela believes Abram teaches his siblings to empathize with other people who might be different.

Cecilie
Lundgreen

1973–PRESENT

Professional Golfer, Convert, and Youth Leader

"If thou wilt do good, yea, and hold out faithful to the end, thou shalt be saved in the kingdom of God, which is the greatest of all the gifts of God." **DOCTRINE AND COVENANTS 6:13**

NEEDING A MIRACLE

Cecilie prayed for a miracle. As she sat by the bedside of her mom, who was lying comatose, Cecilie prayed to God and begged, "Tell me what to do. I can't live without her." Cecilie's mom had fallen ill when a tingling in her hands suddenly led to paralysis and a coma. She had suffered an aneurism, and the doctors tried everything they could to help her but to no avail.[1] Cecilie felt like her mom's life rested in God's hands. Although she had not yet joined The Church of Jesus Christ of Latter-day Saints, Cecilie had been studying the gospel with the missionaries serving in her homeland of Norway, and she was beginning to believe in miracles. She believed that God could save her mom.

Ellen Tveter was more than Cecilie's mom. She was her best friend—her "angel, refuge, and safe place." Ellen had done every-thing in her power to provide a loving and supportive home for Cecilie. After leaving an unhappy and abusive marriage, Ellen raised her two children on her own because Cecilie's biological father couldn't pay for child support. She encouraged Cecilie to obtain a college education, to pursue her dreams of becoming a professional golfer, and to work hard by "doing it right." Ellen meant everything to Cecilie, and she didn't want God to take her mom away from her.

Cecilie asked the missionaries to give her mom a blessing of healing. Because her extended family vehemently opposed her affiliation with the Church, Cecilie had to sneak the missionaries into the ICU late at night with their mission president's permission. As the missionaries were ushered into the hospital room, Cecilie thought that everything would be all right and that the elders would pronounce a miraculous blessing upon her mom.

NO NEED FOR RELIGION

Cecilie hadn't always believed in miracles. In fact, she hadn't always believed in God. With her busy career, she thought she didn't have the time for religion. Cecilie had started playing golf when she was eleven years old. She discovered not only that she liked the sport but that she was good at it too. By the time she was fifteen years old, Cecilie had made the Norwegian national golf team, and by her fourth year of college, she had progressed from an amateur to a professional golfer. In 1999, she joined the Ladies European Tour and traveled the world, representing her country in golf tournaments. Religion was far from Cecilie's mind. She no longer wanted her family to be associated with unhappiness, abuse, and addiction, but she didn't think God or religion would help her achieve such a feat. Rather, she believed her fame and exciting career would change her family's image.

> Cecilie's mom taught her the importance of hard work, integrity, and independence. Ellen's example led Cecilie to adopt the motto "Do it right."

Despite the success of her career, Cecilie's life was peppered with tragedies that left her reeling.

When she was twenty years old, her biological father died due to complications from his alcoholism. The following year, Cecilie's best friend died. Another friend with whom she played golf on the national team died of cancer when he was just eighteen years old. And then her friend's young daughter was killed when she was struck by lightning. Cecilie felt angry. She didn't understand why these tragedies had occurred. She felt like she had been left completely in the dark until she met two women during her golfing tour: Reeve, a coach from Zimbabwe, and Laurette, a golfer from South Africa.

Cecilie knew there was something different about these women. For one thing, they listened to religious music during their travel, and they filled their mini fridge with food so they wouldn't have to purchase anything on Sundays. When Reeve asked Cecilie if she believed in God, Cecilie responded with pain and confusion as she told the coach about the friends and family she had recently lost. Reeve took out a napkin, diagrammed the plan of salvation, and began to tell Cecilie about the gospel

Cecilie on the golf course

as taught in The Church of Jesus Christ of Latter-day Saints. As Cecilie traveled with Reeve and Laurette, she learned more about the Church. She went to a family home evening at her friend's house, where she said her first prayer; attended a fast and testimony meeting; and helped in the Primary.

Cecilie was determined to figure out for herself if joining the Church was the right decision. When her family learned about her associations with the missionaries, they were unhappy. Cecilie's grandmother was convinced that she was joining a cult, but her mom trusted her daughter to make her own decisions. Cecilie knew she could count on her mom's support, which was one reason the threat of losing her was terrifying. With her mom on the brink between life and death, Cecilie turned her heart heavenward and entreated God for a miracle.

EMBRACING THE FUTURE WITH FAITH

Cecilie waited with bated breath as the missionaries laid their hands on her mom's head to bless her. The elder who offered the blessing said, "The Lord loves you. It's time to come home." Cecilie wasn't even sure if she believed what the elder had just said, but she felt a sense of peace knowing she had done everything that she could for her mom. The doctors decided to turn off Ellen's respirator, and Cecilie sat with her mom and held her hand until she died.

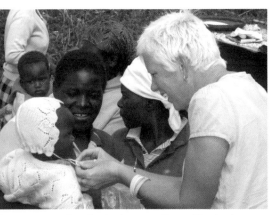

Cecilie helps run Eyes4Zimbabwe, a nonprofit that provides cataract surgery for families in Zimbabwe.

It was the worst day of Cecilie's life, and she missed her mom terribly. But she also remembered what she had learned about the plan of salvation and needed to know if what her friends and the missionaries had taught her was true. During this period of grief and despair, Cecilie's testimony of the gospel grew, and she felt the comforting assurance that the Church was true. On November 14, 2002, just two weeks after her mom's funeral, Cecilie was baptized a member of The Church of Jesus Christ of Latter-day Saints. Her family was furious and assumed she had made a hasty decision that was motivated by grief, but Cecilie felt she had made the best decision of her life.

When Cecilie became a member of the Church, she wanted to be "all in." It was challenging to get back into golfing following her mom's death, but when she did, she was no longer after the titles, trophies, and prestige. Instead, she was determined to share her love for the gospel and to be a righteous example to others, like Reeve and Laurette had been to her. Cecilie worked to be worthy of a temple recommend, and in 2009, she was sealed to her parents in the Stockholm Sweden Temple.

Cecilie's mom was saved, but not in the way she had initially desired or expected. Ellen was saved eternally because her daughter performed saving ordinances and trusted in God's promise of eternal families. Cecilie continues to be "all in" and strives to be worthy of her temple recommend. She has served with the Young Women for thirteen years and has taught virtual seminary for youth living all over Norway for six years. Cecilie loves the teenagers she serves and believes that she can truly see them—their troubles, their trials, and their uncertainties. She tells them her story to help them know that although they might not understand the challenges they'll face in life, they have a divine destiny, and ultimately, God's plan is good.

> Because of her callings, Cecilie feels like a second mother to over one hundred teenagers. She believes God has entrusted her with helping them understand their divine identity.

133

Melissa Wei-Tsing Inouye

1979–PRESENT

Scholar Battling Cancer

"Take therefore no thought for the morrow, for the morrow shall take thought for the things of itself. Sufficient is the day unto the evil thereof." **3 NEPHI 13:34**

A CLOSET INTERVIEW

For what felt like the umpteenth time, Melissa prepared a meal for her family, packed it up, and rode a bus with her four children to meet her husband, Joseph, for dinner in his office building's food court. Joseph worked at a prestigious law firm in Hong Kong, and his hours were less than ideal. On early nights, he came home at 10:00 p.m. Other nights, he came home at midnight. And on late nights, he came home at 2:00 a.m. or even later. This schedule was taxing, and the family determined that it wasn't sustainable. A change was in order, and Melissa soon found herself in the job market.

Melissa applied for a handful of university positions. She had earned a PhD in East Asian languages and civilizations from Harvard University

Melissa and her husband, Joseph

135

Melissa served a mission in parts of Asia, where she developed "huge love" for the people in her ward, as well as strangers around her. She called this love her "superpower."

and had kept her foot in the door of academia by teaching a class at the University of Hong Kong and presenting at the occasional conference. While applying for jobs, however, Melissa was continually met with rejection until one university, the University of Auckland, requested a video interview with her. Melissa didn't have a formal office space, so she completed her job interview in the closet of a storage area on the University of Hong Kong campus. Despite her unconventional location, the hiring committee thought she was the right candidate and offered Melissa her first full-time job.

As a fourth-generation Chinese-Japanese American, Melissa was no stranger to moving or living abroad. She had grown accustomed to the different environments and worldviews in various parts of Asia.[1] But New Zealand was new territory, and it felt so far away from—well, everyone and everything. The family considered the move with some trepidation, but a new adventure and the promise of seeing sheep and glowworms were too good to refuse. Melissa accepted the position at the university, and the family moved to Auckland in 2014.

"CANCER IS BIG AND SCARY"

Melissa initially thought her new position would be a two-year gig, but the family fell in love with New Zealand and decided to stay long-term. Their home remained in a perpetual state of renovation, but they enjoyed gardening, hiking, fishing, and participating in the phenomenal activities their ward family organized, such as the Primary Disco.[2] In May 2017, however, Melissa was diagnosed with colon cancer. In a letter to her loved ones, she wrote, "Cancer is big and scary. Fear and sorrow are real."[3] Melissa felt the stab of fear and uncertainty, especially when she thought of her own mother, who had died of cancer in 2008.[4] She was scheduled for a colectomy as well as an arduous six-month course of chemotherapy.[5]

Melissa and her family at Clearwater Bay, Hong Kong

Melissa at times felt alone as she navigated the throes of cancer, but those who were close to her provided support, compassion, love, and prayers. When Melissa briefly visited Utah for her brother's wedding in August 2017, she and the other women in her family went to the mountains and gathered in a quiet place for prayer. Each woman took turns praying aloud, and they called upon God to bless Melissa and her family. On the following day, Melissa's father and brothers administered a priesthood blessing to her.[6] When it was difficult for Melissa to find peace amid such frightening circumstances, she leaned on her family and her ward members for support. Through their faith,

> Melissa and Joseph have four children, whom they've nicknamed Bean, Sprout, Leaf, and Shoot.

they made the power of God's love real to her, which allowed her to hope and believe. Melissa waited on the Lord, not by doing nothing or biding her time, but by actively trusting in Him.

Melissa and her family love being active and exploring the outdoors.

EMBRACING THE FUTURE WITH FAITH

Surgery and several chemotherapy treatments seemed to keep the cancer at bay, but it made a resurgence in 2019. To access more advanced treatment and live closer to loved ones, Melissa and her family moved to Utah. Despite health challenges, Melissa remains as active as ever in her career. She now works for the Church History Department and contributes to the Global Histories project, a research endeavor that shares stories of faith and sacrifice from Latter-day Saints living around the world. She's published scholarly articles, manuscripts, and a book, *Crossings*—a collection of family newsletters, essays, and personal letters that document lessons learned throughout her life. Her words offer a meaningful feminist and global perspective on faith and Latter-day Saints.

Melissa's career, family experiences, and battle with cancer have helped her attend to the more fundamental questions of her spirituality: "Is there a God? Does my life actually exist in an eternal sense?" Before she was diagnosed with cancer, she took a keen interest in politics and found herself fretting about the political climate and various religious quandaries. But when her prognosis seemed bleak and her fear was at its peak, she didn't care about these things anymore. She said, "What I clung to was this idea that there was a God and that God would help me." Now more than ever, she relies on her faith, her family, and fellow Latter-day Saints who offer her connection, community, ministering, and nourishment. They have been the means by which she finds hope, and she believes this hope has saved her life, time and time again. Melissa's future is full of unknowns, but she embraces her future with faith by asking God for her daily bread: "I don't ask for big chunks of stuff . . . that hasn't worked for me, so I ask for the day's support, help, and strength."

Yvonne Baraketse Nsabimana

1981–PRESENT

Genocide Survivor and Founder of Nonprofit Organization

"For I know that my redeemer liveth, and that he shall stand at the latter day upon the earth." JOB 19:25

THE WAR IN RWANDA

On October 1, 1990, only two days before Yvonne's ninth birthday, a civil war erupted in Rwanda. Long before the war began, the two major ethnic groups in Rwanda, the Hutus and the Tutsis, had, for decades, been embroiled in tension—there had been uprisings, struggles for independence, and class divisions exacerbated by colonization. This conflict reached a critical point when a group of exiled Tutsis known as the Rwandan Patriotic Front (RPF) invaded Rwanda. Soon, massacres ripped across the country, and many displaced civilians sought refuge.[1] Yvonne was scared. Whenever she heard the clamor of gunshots in the distance, she prayed that God would spare her life. She also prayed for her father, who served as the Rwandan military's chief of staff. She rarely saw him and hoped he'd be safe amid the violence and unrest.

For several years, the war raged on until it came to a head on April 6, 1994. Late in the evening, Yvonne and her family patiently waited for her father to return from a peacekeeping mission, so they could eat dinner together. All of a sudden, they heard a loud explosion unlike anything they'd ever heard before. They had grown accustomed to hearing shooting each day, but this explosion was different. When people went outside to find the source of the explosion, some of them could see scattered debris falling from the sky. Two missiles had struck an airplane carrying the President of Rwanda, the President of Burundi, and ten other people. There were no survivors, and Yvonne's father was one of the passengers in the airplane. At just twelve years old, Yvonne lost her father. The family was devastated, and Yvonne cried harder than she ever had in her life. Her anguish was overwhelming, and she didn't know what would become of her family.

SLOW HEALING

The assassinations sparked a genocide, and chaos erupted. Neighbors took up arms against each other, and mass killings ensued. In just one hundred days, over one million people were slaughtered.[2] Many civilians fled from Rwanda, including Yvonne

Yvonne with her family

and her family. Although they eventually arrived safely in Belgium, Yvonne reeled from shock and trauma. She had lost everything and didn't know how to resume her life after surviving such harrowing experiences. Her mother pushed her to move forward, and Yvonne started attending school in Belgium. She spoke French, but she felt like she couldn't talk to her classmates, much less connect with them. She saw them laughing and playing, and she couldn't fathom how they could possibly be happy when she had just experienced the worst weeks of her life.

Yvonne also lost faith in God. If there was a God, she couldn't understand why He'd allow such horrible things to happen—the war, her father's death, the massacres. These young teenage years were the darkest period of Yvonne's life, and in her despair and anger, she decided to stop praying.[3]

As time passed, healing came slowly. It took two years for Yvonne to be able to talk to her classmates and make friends. She and her sister started a small community group where they danced and sang the songs from Rwandan villages. This group, the music, and the dances were healing. They helped her celebrate her identity, cope with trauma, and move forward. In addition to embracing the support of this community, Yvonne eventually invited religion back into her life.

Her boyfriend, Jacques, whom she later married, was also a Rwandan refugee, and he had found peace when he converted to The Church of Jesus Christ of Latter-day Saints. They attended a sacrament meeting together in Brussels, and Yvonne was touched as she saw members of the congregation bear testimony of Heavenly Father and Jesus Christ. She felt that this church was different from others, so she began meeting with the missionaries at the end of 1999. She asked them question after question, and the sister missionaries guided her through gospel lessons, but Yvonne still felt uncertain. After about two years of teaching Yvonne the gospel, the sisters started one lesson with a different approach. They began to sing "I Know That My Redeemer Lives," and every single word resonated with Yvonne and "completely removed the ice" that was on her heart. Yvonne chose to be baptized in 2001,

Yvonne was a refugee for a second time when Hurricane Katrina struck in 2005. Observing the work of refugee and humanitarian organizations inspired her to pursue a degree in public administration.

and the decision changed her life. She realized that she had a Savior who had died for her. She felt like her humanity had been restored, and she learned that forgiveness could help her look to the future with brighter hope.

EMBRACING THE FUTURE WITH FAITH

On April 6, 2009, twenty-five years after her father's death, Yvonne's family and close friends met in Belgium where they held a special Mass. Yvonne's family is Catholic, and they wanted to commemorate her father's life, as well as the lives of those who were killed during the genocide. As the family gathered for prayer, Yvonne thought of her nieces and nephews who were playing outside. She kept having the thought: "Call the kids. The kids have got to be here." Yvonne's father loved children, and she thought of how he'd laugh, dance, and play with the children in the villages he visited. Yvonne gathered her nieces and nephews one by one, and they all sat around the portrait of her father. They took a family picture, and Yvonne offered the prayer. The presence of the Spirit was unmistakable when she realized she had prayed at the exact minute and hour her father had died twenty-five years earlier.

Dancing helps Yvonne celebrate her identity.

Now, Yvonne lives in Utah with her husband and four children. She's often reflected on how and why she survived a terrible genocide while thousands of others lost their lives. She believes that God has a mission for her, so she's dedicated her life to serving His children. Not only has she helped refugees and underprivileged families, but she also founded the Ngoma Y'Africa Cultural Center in Provo, a nonprofit organization that empowers Black students, helps them celebrate their cultural identity, and creates understanding between different cultures. Her family has also written a book called *Résilience*, which tells her father's story as well as lessons learned from his life.[4] Yvonne's service allows her to embrace her identity, honor her father's legacy, and follow God's plan for her. She knows that her life isn't free from challenges, but she feels uplifted when she completely surrenders to God and trusts His love for her. Yvonne relies on faith, which she believes is a "power . . . that will never go away."

Yvonne and fellow community members performed an African dance at the Church's "Be One" celebration, which marked the fortieth anniversary of the 1978 revelation on the priesthood.

Melissa Te'o
Laurenson

1990–PRESENT

Devoted Caregiver and Missionary

"In my distress I called upon the Lord, and cried unto my God: he heard my voice out of his temple, and my cry came before him, even into his ears." **PSALM 18:6**

A DAUGHTER'S PURPOSE

It was Melissa's first semester of college at Waikato University in Hamilton, New Zealand.[1] She was in the middle of an exam prep class when her older brother called, saying that she needed to return home to Auckland immediately. Their mother, Melesa Te'o, had fallen ill, and she needed someone to take care of her. Although Melissa was concerned about her mom, she also felt frustrated. She didn't want to leave the university when she was so close to finishing her semester, and she wondered why her three older brothers couldn't take care of their mom.[2] Once Melissa finished her final exams, she moved back home to help her mom. Initially, Melissa was able to earn money by working night shifts at Burger King because her mom was still able to perform small tasks independently. But Melesa's condition worsened. She was diagnosed with cancer, and she refused chemotherapy because she saw how painful the treatment was for other people. Melissa quit her job in order to become her mom's full-time caregiver. Melissa cooked for her, bathed her, changed her diapers, and managed her medications.

Melissa had been adopted into her family when she was just

two months old, and in harmony with Samoan custom, as the only daughter, she cared for her elders. Melissa did her best to honor this cultural tradition, but she also resented the obligation. Her brothers did not share the responsibility of caring for their mother like Melissa thought they could, while she had to put her life plans on hold. She was unhappy and wanted someone to know how she felt. She often looked sad or tired, and her mom could see it in her face.

One day, as Melissa assisted her mom, Melesa looked at her daughter with tears in her eyes and said, "I'm sorry." Upon hearing this apology, Melissa thought her heart would break. She had always known her mom to be a strong and independent woman, but in that moment, her mom was feeling helpless, undignified, and vulnerable. Melissa tried to empathize with her mom and imagine what it'd be like to be stuck in bed all day, unable to do anything for herself. Melissa decided that if she was going to care for her mom, she was going to do it with the right attitude. She made sure that her actions and disposition reflected the love she had for her mom. She continued to care for her mom until Melesa died in 2011.

SERVING THE PEOPLE OF SAMOA

This was not the first parent Melissa had lost. Her dad, Numiamasasulu Te'o, had died of a heart attack just three years earlier when she was still in high school. Now with both of her parents gone, Melissa felt alone and lost. While praying, she cried aloud and called out to her parents because she missed them. Many families helped Melissa, providing her with support, companionship, and housing until she settled in with relatives. Although her grief felt heavy and painful, Melissa remembered that she had received multiple impressions to serve a mission while her mom had been ill. Such impressions filled her mind once again, but she wondered if she even fit the mold of a missionary. She believed her knowledge of the gospel was inadequate, and she felt like she attended church primarily to socialize with friends, but Melissa was determined to prepare herself so she'd be worthy to devote eighteen months of her life to the Lord.

Melissa (far left) loved her mission and the people she served. Samoa feels like another home to her.

There was just one roadblock preventing Melissa from serving a mission. She struggled to save money, and she didn't have the finances for a mission. She felt frustrated and hopeless, but God blessed her with a miracle. Melissa became especially close with the Fitisemanu family in her ward. Jay and Kim Fitisemanu told Melissa that they'd pay for her mission and that she didn't need to worry about a thing. With their kindness and generosity, she was able to serve in the Samoa Apia Mission in 2015.

Melissa loved her mission. She loved the people she served, learned daily from her companions, and studied the Book of Mormon in greater detail than she ever had before. Although Melissa enjoyed visiting with many different people, she particularly relished working with a woman named Leva'aia Levao, who lived on the isolated Manu'a Islands. Leva'aia was different from other investigators. She was partially deaf and partially blind, so teaching

While on her mission, Melissa loved eating oka, a Samoan dish made with raw fish. It reminded her of when her dad gave her the tail of the last fish he caught while fishing.

her the gospel was challenging. The missionaries took turns teaching Leva'aia and helped her read the Book of Mormon. Although they made slow progress, Leva'aia eventually chose to be baptized. Melissa was overjoyed when Leva'aia joined the Church and appreciated the important lesson she had learned—that to teach like the Savior, she needed to adjust her teaching methods to meet the unique needs of God's children.

EMBRACING THE FUTURE WITH FAITH

Melissa returned home from her mission in 2017. She wanted to continue teaching, so she accepted a job at the Missionary Training Center in Auckland. Melissa loves helping missionaries learn their lessons, their routines, and their purpose. Melissa even met her future husband, Alma Laurenson, at the MTC, and they were mar-

Melissa with her husband, Alma, and their children

ried in 2018. Melissa and Alma had three children, including twins, in a two-year period. Although her schedule is jam-packed, Melissa tries to put her family first and knows that as she teaches her family gospel truths, she is building up the kingdom of God.

As Melissa looks to the future, she takes it day by day: "If I think of the next five years, I think I'd break!" While her past was filled with uncertainty and grief because of the loss of her parents, she has learned the value of making choices based on faith rather than fear. In order to do that, she reminds herself, "God really is in control no matter how bad my circumstances are. . . .

LEVA'AIA LEVAO

While on her mission, Melissa felt privileged to teach Leva'aia Levao, an investigator who lived on Olosega, a small island in the Manu'a Islands of American Samoa. Life wasn't easy for Leva'aia due to several physical limitations. She was partially deaf and blind, and she wore a prosthetic leg because her own had to be amputated. Leva'aia developed boils on her eyes, which caused them to bleed. When three missionaries approached her and tried to teach her about the gospel, Leva'aia struggled to comprehend what the elders were saying, but she understood their message when they showed her a picture of Christ healing a woman. She accepted a blessing of healing from the missionaries, and the following morning, the boils on her eyes were gone.

Leva'aia Levao, one of Melissa's most memorable investigators

Leva'aia began meeting with the missionaries, which is how she eventually met Melissa, and although lessons progressed slowly, she did her best to read a couple verses of scripture each day. Some members of the community mocked Leva'aia and even tore up her notes when they learned about her investigation, but she persisted and was eventually baptized. Leva'aia was called the "heart of the Church on Olosega" because of the profound influence she had on others. Her husband and three children chose to be baptized, and she was called as the Relief Society president of her branch.[3]

Notes

INTRODUCTION

Epigraph: Russell M. Nelson, "Embrace the Future with Faith," *Liahona*, November 2020, https://www.churchofjesuschrist.org/study /liahona/2020/11/37nelson?lang=eng.

1. David B. Haight, "The Primary Enriches the Lives of Children," *Ensign*, April 1978, https://www.churchofjesuschrist.org/study /general-conference/1978/04/the-primary -enriches-the-lives-of-children?lang=eng; Quentin L. Cook, "The Songs They Could Not Sing," *Ensign*, November 2011, https://www .churchofjesuschrist.org/study/ensign /2011/11/sunday-afternoon-session/the -songs-they-could-not-sing?lang=eng.

SHE DEFENDED: AMANDA BARNES SMITH

1. "Hawn's (Haun's) Mill, Caldwell County, Missouri," Ensign Peak Foundation, https:// ensignpeakfoundation.org/hauns-mill-2/; Gerald Lund, "The Revelation That Saved One Boy during the Haun's Mill Massacre," LDSLiving, October 30, 2018, https://www .ldsliving.com/the-revelation-that-saved -one-boy-shot-during-the-hauns-mill -massacre/s/89615.

2. Lund, "Revelation That Saved One Boy"; "Hawn's Mill Massacre," Church History, The Church of Jesus Christ of Latter-day Saints, https://www.churchofjesuschrist.org /study/history/topics/hawns-mill -massacre?lang=eng.

3. "Hawn's (Haun's) Mill, Caldwell County, Missouri."

4. Lund, "Revelation That Saved One Boy"; "Hawn's Mill Massacre"; Alexander L. Baugh, "A Rare Account of the Haun's Mill Massacre: The Reminiscence of Willard Gilbert Smith," *Mormon Historical Studies* 8, nos. 1–2 (Spring–Fall 2007): 166–67.

5. "Amanda Barnes Smith," Church History, The Church of Jesus Christ of Latter-day Saints, https://www.churchofjesuschrist .org/study/history/topics/amanda-barnes -smith?lang=eng.

6. Edward W. Tullidge, *The Women of Mormondom* (New York, New York: Oxford University Library, 1877), 129–32; "Amanda Barnes Smith," Wikipedia, https:// en.wikipedia.org/wiki/Amanda_Barnes _Smith.

7. "Amanda Barnes Smith," Church History; "Amanda Barnes Smith," Wikipedia; Susa Young Gates, *Heroines of "Mormondom": The Second Book of the Noble Women's Lives Series* (Salt Lake City: Juvenile Instructor Office, 1884), 70–72.

8. "Alma Lamoni Smith," Find a Grave, https://www.findagrave.com/memorial/17763937/alma-lamoni-smith; Richard L. Jensen, "Forgotten Relief Societies," *Dialogue: A Journal of Mormon Thought* 16, no. 1 (Spring 1983): 109.

9. "Amanda Barnes Smith," Church History.

Callout, p. 9: Tullidge, *Women of Mormondom*, 129–30.

Callout, p. 10: Emmeline B. Wells, "Amanda Smith," *Woman's Exponent* 10, no. 5 (August 1, 1881): 37.

SHE DREAMED: MARY DUNSTER CHITTENDEN

1. "A Dream Fulfilled," Global Histories, The Church of Jesus Christ of Latter-day Saints, https://www.churchofjesuschrist.org/study/history/global-histories/australia/stories-of-faith/au-02-a-dream-fulfilled?lang=eng; Marjorie B. Newton, "Australia's Pioneer Saints," *Ensign*, February 1997, https://www.churchofjesuschrist.org/study/ensign/1997/02/australias-pioneer-saints?lang=eng.

2. Susa Young Gates, *Heroines of "Mormondom": The Second Book of the Noble Women's Lives Series* (Salt Lake City: Juvenile Instructor Office, 1884), 35.

3. "Dream Fulfilled."

4. "Dream Fulfilled"; Gates, *Heroines of "Mormondom,"* 37–38; Newton, "Australia's Pioneer Saints."

5. Gates, *Heroines of "Mormondom,"* 40–44.

6. "Dream Fulfilled"; Gates, *Heroines of "Mormondom,"* 51, 53-55, 63; "Mary Dunster Chittenden," Find a Grave, last modified November 13, 2009, https://www.findagrave.com/memorial/44297447/mary-chittenden.

7. Gates, *Heroines of "Mormondom,"* 63–64.

8. "Number of LDS Temples by Year," Family Locket, https://familylocket.com/wp-content/uploads/2016/04/temple-list-by-year-2-pages.pdf.

9. Gates, *Heroines of "Mormondom,"* 65.

10. "Mary Dunster Chittenden."

11. "Dream Fulfilled"; Newton, "Australia's Pioneer Saints."

Callout, p. 13: Gates, *Heroines of "Mormondom,"* 65.

Callout, p. 15: Gates, *Heroines of "Mormondom,"* 63.

Callout, p. 16: Gates, *Heroines of "Mormondom,"* 65.

SHE LED: AURELIA SPENCER ROGERS

1. Aurelia S. Rogers, *Life Sketches of Orson Spencer and Others, and History of Primary Work* (Salt Lake City: George Q. Cannon & Sons, 1898), 47, 71.

2. David B. Haight, "The Primary Enriches the Lives of Children," *Ensign*, April 1978, https://www.churchofjesuschrist.org/study/general-conference/1978/04/the-primary-enriches-the-lives-of-children?lang=eng; Rogers, *Life Sketches*, 48–51, 87.

3. Rogers, *Life Sketches*, 15–16, 31–32.

4. Haight, "Primary Enriches the Lives of Children"; Rogers, *Life Sketches*, 87.

5. Susan Easton Black and Mary Jane Woodger, *Women of Character: Profiles of 100 Prominent LDS Women* (American Fork, UT: Covenant Communications, 2011), 262; Haight, "Primary Enriches the Lives of Children"; Rogers, *Life Sketches*, 76–80, 120–22.

6. Haight, "Primary Enriches the Lives of Children"; Rogers, *Life Sketches*, 163–64.

7. "A History of the Primary Organization,"

Church History, The Church of Jesus Christ of Latter-day Saints, https://history.churchof jesuschrist.org/content/a-history-of-the -primary-organization?lang=eng; Mari-anne H. Prescott, "Primary Celebrates 140 Years This Month," Church News, https:// www.churchofjesuschrist.org/church /news/primary-celebrates-140-years-this -month?lang=eng; Haight, "Primary Enriches the Lives of Children"; Rogers, *Life Sketches*, 261.

8. Rogers, *Life Sketches*, 266–73.

9. "Aurelia Read Spencer," FamilySearch, https://www.familysearch.org/tree/person /details/KWJ6-C8S.

10. Prescott, "Primary Celebrates 140 Years."

11. Rogers, *Life Sketches*, 301–7.

12. "Aurelia Read Spencer"; Rogers, *Life Sketches*, 331.

Callout, p. 19: Rogers, *Life Sketches*, 49–50.

Callout, p. 21: Rogers, *Life Sketches*, 126.

Callout, p. 22: Rogers, *Life Sketches*, iii.

SHE ENDURED: LILIA WAHAPAA KANEIHALAU

1. Clarice B. Taylor, "Wahappa—A Kauai Kuaaina," *Honolulu Star-Bulletin*, May 25, 1940, https://www.newspapers.com /clip/22422674/honolulu-star-bulletin/.

2. Hank Soboleski, "Hawaiian Centenar-ian Mrs. Lilia Wahapaa Kaneihalau," *The Garden Island*, June 11, 2017, https://www .thegardenisland.com/2017/06/11/lifestyles /hawaiian-centenarian-mrs-lilia-wahapaa -kaneihalau/.

3. Taylor, "Wahappa"; "Hawaiian Language," Wikipedia, last modified January 4, 2022, https://en.wikipedia.org/wiki/Hawaiian _language.

4. See Lance Chase, "If at First You Don't Suc-ceed: The Beginnings of Mormon Missionary Work on Kauai, 1850–54," *Mormon Pacific Historical Society* 16 (1995): 25; Sharon Had-dock, "Hawaii: Persevere and 'Be Blessed,'" *Deseret News*, July 18, 2009, https://www .deseret.com/2009/7/18/20329248/hawaii -persevere-and-be-blessed.

5. Chase, "If at First You Don't Succeed," 25–27.

6. Susan Easton Black and Mary Jane Wood-ger, *Women of Character: Profiles of 100 Prominent LDS Women* (American Fork, UT: Covenant Communications, 2011), 346.

7. Black and Woodger, *Women of Character*, 347.

8. "A Life That Spans the Mormon Era," The Hawaiian Mission in Review, n.d., digital file, 34.

9. Black and Woodger, *Women of Character*, 347.

10. Virginia Bennett Hill, "Wahapaa, 106, to Get Her First Plane Ride," *Honolulu Star-Bulletin*, April 3, 1942, https://www.newspapers.com /clip/22422649/106-yr-old4/.

11. "Life That Spans the Mormon Era," 34.

12. "Life That Spans the Mormon Era," 36.

13. Black and Woodger, *Women of Character*, 348.

14. "Hawaii—Facts and Statistics," Newsroom, The Church of Jesus Christ of Latter-day Saints, https://newsroom.churchofjesus christ.org/facts-and-statistics/state/hawaii.

15. "Life That Spans the Mormon Era," 36.

Callout, p. 26: Black and Woodger, *Women of Character*, 346.

Callout, p. 28: Hill, "Wahapaa."

SHE PRAYED: ANNIE GILLIES PARKER

1. Lula Parker Betenson, *Butch Cassidy, My Brother* (Provo, UT: Brigham Young University Press, 1975), 7, 10–11; "Van Vleet Cabin in Circleville, UT Boyhood Home of Butch Cassidy," Maximillian Parker, FamilySearch, https://www.familysearch.org/tree/person/memories/KWCR-J2F.

2. Betenson, *Butch Cassidy*, 30, 34, 38, 55, 164, 167–68, 237.

3. Elizabeth Nix, "6 Things You May Not Know about Butch Cassidy," History, updated January 17, 2020, https://www.history.com/news/6-things-you-might-not-know-about-butch-cassidy; "Annie Campbell Gillies," FamilySearch, https://ancestors.familysearch.org/en/KWCR-J2N/ann-campbell-gillies-1847-1905; Betenson, *Butch Cassidy*, 25, 30.

4. "Annie Campbell Gillies"; Betenson, *Butch Cassidy*, 25, 27, 29, 31.

5. "Van Vleet Cabin"; Betenson, *Butch Cassidy*, xiii, 34, 38.

6. "Van Vleet Cabin"; Betenson, *Butch Cassidy*, 40–42.

7. "Butch Cassidy," Wikipedia, last modified April 13, 2022, 19:40, https://en.wikipedia.org/wiki/Butch_Cassidy; Betenson, *Butch Cassidy*, 48–49.

8. "Van Vleet Cabin"; Betenson, *Butch Cassidy*, 36, 42–48, 51, 55, 182, 225.

9. Hadley Meares, "Butch Cassidy and the Sundance Kid: The True Story of the Famous Outlaws," Biography, updated September 8, 2020, https://www.biography.com/news/butch-cassidy-sundance-kid-real-story; "Annie Campbell Gillies"; "Van Vleet Cabin"; Betenson, *Butch Cassidy*, 64–65.

10. Betenson, *Butch Cassidy*, 34, 36.

11. Betenson, *Butch Cassidy*, 34, 38–39, 164, 167, 181, 225–28, 231, 237.

12. "Van Vleet Cabin"; Betenson, *Butch Cassidy*, 36–37, 42, 47, 51, 164, 167, 228, 237.

Callout, p. 32: Betenson, *Butch Cassidy*, 225.

Callout, p. 35: Betenson, *Butch Cassidy*, 167.

SHE ENVISIONED: MARTHA ANN STEVENS HOWELL

1. Brittany Chapman Nash and Richard E. Turley Jr., eds., *Women of Faith in the Latter Days*, vol. 4, *1871–1900* (Salt Lake City: Deseret Book, 2017), 103–4, 322; "Race and the Priesthood," Gospel Topics Essays, The Church of Jesus Christ of Latter-day Saints, https://www.churchofjesuschrist.org/study/manual/gospel-topics-essays/race-and-the-priesthood?lang=eng.

2. "Martha Ann Jane Stevens Perkins Howell," MormonWiki, last modified June 24, 2021, https://www.mormonwiki.com/Martha_Ann_Jane_Stevens_Perkins_Howell; Margaret Blair Young, "Abner Leonard Howell (1877–1966)," BlackPast, https://www.blackpast.org/african-american-history/howell-abner-leonard-1877-1966/; Nash and Turley, *Women*, 97, 99–100, 102–4.

3. "Green Flake," Century of Black Mormons, J. Willard Marriott Library, University of Utah, https://exhibits.lib.utah.edu/s/century-of-black-mormons/page/flake-green#?#_ftn9&cv=3&xywh=346%2C137%2C3211%2C1472.

4. "Martha Ann Jane Stevens Perkins Howell"; Nash and Turley, *Women*, 97–98, 102–3, 107.

5. Nash and Turley, *Women*, 104.

6. Kate B. Carter, *The Story of the Negro Pioneer* (Salt Lake City: Daughters of Utah Pioneers, 1965), 59.

7. Nash and Turley, *Women*, 104–7.

8. Nash and Turley, *Women*, 107; "Martha Ann Jane Stevens Perkins Howell."

9. Nash and Turley, *Women*, 107.

10. Nash and Turley, *Women*, 97–102; Margaret Blair Young, "The Black Woman Who Served an Unprecedented Church Mission to Help Reduce Segregation, Prejudice in the Church," *LDS Living*, February 19, 2019, ldsliving.com/the-black-woman-who -served-an-unprecedented-church -mission-to-help-reduce-segregation -prejudice-in-the-church/s/90299.

11. Nash and Turley, *Women*, 97, 102.

12. Nash and Turley, *Women*, 101.

13. Michael Aguirre, "Ruffin Bridgeforth (1923–1997)," BlackPast, last modified August 29, 2016, https://www.blackpast .org/african-american-history/people -african-american-history/bridgeforth -ruffin-1923-1997/.

14. "History," Utah Area Genesis Group of The Church of Jesus Christ of Latter-day Saints, https://www.ldsgenesisgroup.org/#history.

15. Tad Walch, "LDS Church Reorganizes Genesis Group Leadership," *Deseret News*, January 8, 2018, https://www.deseret.com /2018/1/8/20637984/lds-church-re organizes-genesis-group-leadership.

16. "The Genesis Group Gathers on Temple Square to Celebrate 50 Years since Its Creation," Newsroom, The Church of Jesus Christ of Latter-day Saints, October 23, 2021, https://newsroom.churchofjesuschrist.org /article/genesis-group-50-years.

Callout, p. 37: Nash and Turley, *Women*, 100.

Callout, p. 39: Nash and Turley, *Women*, 100.

SHE PERSEVERED: AUGUSTE KUHLMANN LIPPELT

1. "Aftermath of World War I and the Rise of Nazism, 1918–1933," United States Holocaust Memorial Museum, https://www.ushmm .org/learn/holocaust/path-to-nazi -genocide/chapter-1/aftermath-of-world -war-i-and-the-rise-of-nazism-1918-1933.

2. Ana C. Soli, "Brazil: Born of Spiritual Beginnings," *Deseret News*, December 17, 2004, https://www.thechurchnews.com/archives /2004-12-18/brazil-born-of-spiritual -beginnings-93605.

3. "Auguste Kuhlmann Lippelt," FamilySearch, https://www.familysearch.org/tree/person /details/K244-NYK; Soli, "Brazil."

4. "Here the Mormons Will Not Find Me," Global Histories, The Church of Jesus Christ of Latter-day Saints, https://www .churchofjesuschrist.org/study/history /global-histories/brazil/stories-of-faith/br -01-here-the-mormons-will-not-find-me ?lang=eng; Rubens L. DaSilva, "Os Mormons em Santa Catarina: Origins, conflitos e desenvolvimento" [The Mormons in Santa Catarina: Origins, Conflicts and Development] (master's diss., Mackenzie Presbyterian University, 2008), https:// docplayer.com.br/48041176-Universidade -presbiteriana-mackenzie-rubens-lima -da-silva-mestrado-em-ciencias-da -religiao.html#show_full_text.

5. DaSilva, "Mormons in Santa Catarina"; Soli, "Brazil"; Celso Sanches and Cristina Sanches, "Roots and Branches of the Church in Brazil: The Eighty Years of the Brazilian Missions," The Church of Jesus Christ of Latter-day Saints, Brazil, https:// br-aigrejadejesuscristo-org.translate .goog/raizes-e-ramos-no-brasilos -oitenta-anos-das-missoes-brasileiras ?_x_tr_sl=pt&_x_tr_tl=en&_x_tr_hl=en -US&_x_tr_pto=sc.

6. "Brazil—Facts and Statistics," Newsroom, The Church of Jesus Christ of Latter-day Saints, https://newsroom.churchofjesuschrist.org /facts-and-statistics/country/brazil.

7. Soli, "Brazil."

8. "Auguste Kuhlmann Lippelt"; "Here the Mormons Will Not Find Me."

9. DaSilva, "Mormons in Santa Catarina"; "Here the Mormons Will Not Find Me."

10. DaSilva, "The Mormons in Santa Catarina"

11. "Brazil—Facts and Statistics."

12. Soli, "Brazil."

13. Soli, "Brazil."

SHE HELPED: IRENE COLVIN CORBETT

1. Heather Hayes, "Why Was Utah's Only *Titanic* Passenger Not among the Survivors?" *Salt Lake Magazine*, March 15, 2021, https://www.saltlakemagazine.com/irene-corbett-titanic-passenger/.

2. Glen Warchol, "Tragic Tale of Provo Woman Links Utah, Titanic Fate," *Salt Lake Tribune*, April 15, 2012, https://archive.sltrib.com/article.php?id=53886783&itype=cmsid#gallery-carousel-446996; Hayes, "Utah's Only *Titanic* Passenger."

3. Don Corbett (grandson of Irene Corbett), phone interview with author Emily Cushing, November 29, 2021. Don's father, Mack Corbett, was Irene's youngest son. Many of Irene's photographs, letters, and postcards are in Don's possession.

4. "Irene Corbett," Encyclopedia Titanica, last updated January 14, 2016, https://encyclopedia-titanica.org/titanic-victim/irene-corbett.html; Hayes, "Utah's Only *Titanic* Passenger"; Warchol, "Tragic Tale."

5. Corbett, interview with Cushing.

6. Warchol, "Tragic Tale"; Corbett, interview with Cushing.

7. Warchol, "Tragic Tale"; Corbett, interview with Cushing.

Callout, p. 52: Corbett, interview with Cushing.

Callout, p. 53: Hayes, "Utah's Only *Titanic* Passenger"; Corbett, interview with Cushing.

Callout, p. 55: "S.S. Virginian," WikiTree, https://www.wikitree.com/wiki/Space:S.S._Virginian; Warchol, "Tragic Tale."

SHE CONNECTED: HELEN DOWAWISNIMA SEKAQUAPTEWA

1. Helen Sekaquaptewa and Louise Udall, *Me and Mine* (Tucson, AZ: University of Arizona Press, 1969), 92; Laura Redish and Orrin Lewis, "Hopi Indian Fact Sheet," Orrin's Website, http://www.bigorrin.org/hopi_kids.htm.

2. "Hopi," Wikimedia Foundation, last modified April 12, 2022, 21:50, https://en.wikipedia.org/wiki/Hopi; Sekaquaptewa and Udall, *Me and Mine*, 64.

3. FamilySearch, "Helen Dowawisnima," Memories, "The Trail Has Come Full Circle," https://www.familysearch.org/tree/person/memories/KN92-ZGX; Sekaquaptewa and Udall, *Me and Mine*, 12, 92, 93, 107–8.

4. FamilySearch, "Helen Dowawisnima," Memories, "Honored Guest," https://www.familysearch.org/tree/person/memories/KN92-ZGX; Sekaquaptewa and Udall, *Me and Mine*, 91–93, 104–5.

5. FamilySearch, "Honored Guest"; Sekaquaptewa and Udall, *Me and Mine*, 91–93, 144–45.

6. Sekaquaptewa and Udall, *Me and Mine*, 140–41.

7. Sekaquaptewa and Udall, *Me and Mine*, 185–86, 188, 190, 221.

8. Sekaquaptewa and Udall, *Me and Mine*, 144–45, 185–88, 190, 198–99, 221.

9. Sekaquaptewa and Udall, *Me and Mine*, 203.

10. Clarence Barker, "Marriage to Hopi Indians Is Not for This Life Only," Church News, June

1973, https://www.familysearch.org/tree/person/memories/KN92-ZGX; Sekaquaptewa and Udall, *Me and Mine*, 117–19, 236, 240–42.

11. FamilySearch, "Honored Guest"; Sekaquaptewa and Udall, *Me and Mine*, 243.

12. FamilySearch, "The Trail Has Come Full Circle."

13. "Helen Sekaquaptewa," Arizona Women's Hall of Fame, https://www.azwhf.org/copy-of-clara-m-schell; FamilySearch, "The Trail Has Come Full Circle"; Sekaquaptewa and Udall, *Me and Mine*, 217–18, 245.

14. FamilySearch, "Honored Guest."

15. Sekaquaptewa and Udall, *Me and Mine*, 247; "Helen Sekaquaptewa"; FamilySearch, "The Trail Has Come Full Circle."

Callout, p. 59: Sekaquaptewa and Udall, *Me and Mine*, 243.

Callout, p. 63: Sekaquaptewa and Udall, *Me and Mine*, 245.

SHE UPLIFTED: MAXINE TATE GRIMM

1. *Pete & Maxine: The Grimms' Tale*, directed by Christopher Allen Garcia, (BYU Library Lectures, 2018), YouTube video, 1:32:20, https://www.youtube.com/watch?v=gDhlPDjXQI4.

2. "Anemia, Pernicious," National Organization for Rare Disorders, https://rarediseases.org/rare-diseases/anemia-pernicious/; Garcia, *Grimms' Tale*.

3. Garcia, *Grimms' Tale*.

4. Sheridan R. Sheffield, "'A Genuine Pioneer' in the Philippines," Church News, February 1993, https://www.thechurchnews.com/archives/1993-02-13/a-genuine-pioneer-in-the-philippines-143103; Garcia, *Grimms' Tale*.

5. Garcia, *Grimms' Tale*.

6. Sheffield, "Genuine Pioneer"; Garcia, *Grimms' Tale*.

7. Garcia, *Grimms' Tale*.

8. Pete Grimm (Maxine's son), email to author Emily Cushing, December 18, 2021; Garcia, *Grimms' Tale*.

9. Garcia, *Grimms' Tale*.

10. "The Church of Jesus Christ in the Philippines," Wikipedia, https://en.wikipedia.org/wiki/The_Church_of_Jesus_Christ_of_Latter-day_Saints_in_the_Philippines.

11. "Grimm, Maxine Tate, 1914–2017," Special Collections, Harold B. Lee Library, Brigham Young University, http://archives.lib.byu.edu/agents/people/13143; "The Lord Is Smiling on the Philippines," Global Histories, The Church of Jesus Christ of Latter-day Saints, https://www.churchofjesuschrist.org/study/history/global-histories/philippines/stories-of-faith/ph-01-the-lord-is-smiling-on-the-philippines?lang=eng; Weaver, "Moment."

12. Sheffield, "Genuine Pioneer."

13. "The Lord Is Smiling."

Callout, p. 66: Garcia, *Grimms' Tale*.

Callout, p. 67: Garcia, *Grimms' Tale*.

Callout, p. 68: Pete Grimm (Maxine's son), email to author Emily Cushing, October 17, 2022.

Callout, p. 69: "Philippines," Temples of The Church of Jesus Christ of Latter-day Saints, https://churchofjesuschristtemples.org/statistics/locations/philippines/.

SHE INFLUENCED: CARMEN GALVEZ O'DONNAL

1. John F. O'Donnal, *Pioneer in Guatemala: The Personal History of John Forres O'Donnal, Including the History of the Church of Jesus Christ of Latter-day Saints*

in Guatemala (Yorba Linda, CA: self-pub., Shumway Family History Services, 1997), 32, http://larryrichman.org/wp-content /uploads/pioneer-guatemala-john -odonnal.pdf.

2. "Pioneers in Guatemala," Global Histories, The Church of Jesus Christ of Latter-day Saints, https://www.churchofjesuschrist.org /study/history/global-histories /guatemala/stories-of-faith/gt-01 -pioneers-in-guatemala?lang=eng.

3. O'Donnal, *Pioneer in Guatemala*, 32.

4. Steve Fidel and Chelsea Warren, "Pioneers of a Different Era," *Deseret News*, July 18, 2009, https://www.deseret.com /2009/7/18/20329276/pioneers-of-a -different-era#carmen-g-odonnal-and -john-odonnal-worked-in-guatemala -carmen-was-the-first-guatemalan-to-be -baptized.

5. "Pioneers in Guatemala."

6. "Pioneers in Guatemala."

7. "Pioneers in Guatemala."

8. Ryan Saltzgiver, "Women of Faith: Stories from Global Histories," in *Latter-day Saint Women* (podcast), produced by The Church of Jesus Christ of Latter-day Saints, https:// www.churchofjesuschrist.org/media /collection/latter-day-saint-women -podcasts?lang=eng.

9. Fidel and Warren, "Pioneers of a Different Era."

10. Saltzgiver, "Women of Faith."

11. Saltzgiver, "Women of Faith."

12. "A Brief History of the Church in Guate-mala," Global Histories, The Church of Jesus Christ of Latter-day Saints, https://www. churchofjesuschrist.org/study/history /global-histories/guatemala/gt-overview ?lang=eng.

13. Saltzgiver, "Women of Faith," 15; "A Brief History of the Church in Guatemala."

Callout, p. 73: O'Donnal, *Pioneer in Guatemala*, 303.

Callout, p. 74: Elena O'Donnal (daughter-in-law of Carmen), phone interview with author Emily Cushing, July 22, 2022.

Callout, p. 75: O'Donnal, *Pioneer in Guatemala*, 340–50.

SHE INSPIRED: CHIEKO NISHIMURA OKAZAKI

1. Chieko N. Okazaki, *Lighten Up!* (Salt Lake City: Deseret Book, 1993), 3, 7; Kenneth Alohi Okazaki (son of Chieko Okazaki), phone interview with author Emily Cushing, November 2, 2022.

2. Chieko N. Okazaki, "Cat's Cradle of Kindness," *Ensign*, April 1993, https://www .churchofjesuschrist.org/study/general -conference/1993/04/cats-cradle-of -kindness?lang=eng.

3. "*Kigatsuku* Girl," Global Histories, The Church of Jesus Christ of Latter-day Saints, https://www.churchofjesuschrist.org/study /history/global-histories/hawaii/stories -of-faith/hi-04-kigatsuku-girl?lang=eng; Dennis Lythgoe, "LDS Book Author Was Taught Love, Charity through Buddhist Roots," *Deseret News*, December 29, 2002, https://www.deseret.com/2002/12/29 /19696242/lds-author-okazaki-was-taught -love-charity-through-buddhist-roots.

4. "*Kigatsuku* Girl"; Okazaki, *Lighten Up!*, 3, 7.

5. Okazaki, *Lighten Up!*, 48–50.

6. "*Kigatsuku* Girl."

7. Okazaki, *Lighten Up!*, 4–5.

8. Chieko N. Okazaki, *Being Enough* (Salt Lake City: Bookcraft, 2002), 173; Okazaki, *Lighten Up!*, 4–5.

9. Chieko N. Okazaki, "Baskets and Bottles,"

Ensign, May 1996, https://www.churchof
jesuschrist.org/study/ensign/1996/05
/baskets-and-bottles?lang=eng.

10. Chieko N. Okazaki, "Healing from Sexual
Abuse" (address, Brigham Young University,
Provo, UT, October 23, 2002), https://www
.churchofjesuschrist.org/bc/content/ldsorg
/topics/welfare/pdf/Healing-from-Sexual
-Abuse-Okazaki.pdf.

11. Okazaki, *Lighten Up!*, 3.

Callout, p. 78: Robert Kealiiululani Okazaki (son
of Chieko Okazaki), phone interview with
author Emily Cushing, January 16, 2022;
Okazaki, *Lighten Up!*, 29–30.

Callout, p. 80: "Chieko Okazaki Obituary,"
Deseret News, August 7, 2011, https://www
.legacy.com/us/obituaries/deseretnews
/name/chiekookazaki-obituary?id
=15214849; Okazaki, "Healing from Sexual
Abuse"; Kenneth Okazaki, interview with
Cushing.

Callout, p. 81: "The Mormon Pavilion at the 1970
World's Exposition," Global Histories, The
Church of Jesus Christ of Latter-day Saints,
https://www.churchofjesuschrist.org/study
/history/global-histories/6apan/stories-of
-faith/jp-05-the-mormon-pavilion-at-the
-1970-worlds-exposition?lang=eng.

SHE TAUGHT: ELSIE SREENIVASAM DHARMARAJU

1. "Richard Orran Ashby," Obituaries, *Millard
County Chronicle Progress* (Delta, UT),
November 24, 2017, https://millardccp.com
/obituary-announcements/2597-richard
-orran-ashby.

2. William Kesler Jackson, "Lillian Ashby and
the Dharmarajus: How One Woman Helped
Plant the Church in India," Church History,
The Church of Jesus Christ of Latter-day
Saints, https://history.churchofjesuschrist
.org/content/lillian-ashby-and-the
-dharmarajus?lang=eng.

3. "I Will Establish a Church by Your Hand,"
Global Histories, The Church of Jesus Christ
of Latter-day Saints, https://www.church
ofjesuschrist.org/study/history/global
-histories/india/stories-of-faith/in-03-i-will
-establish-a-church-by-your-hand?lang
=eng; Taunalyn Rutherford, *The Worldwide
Church: Mormonism as a Global Religion*
(Provo, UT: BYU Religious Studies Center;
Salt Lake City: Deseret Book, 2016), 78.

4. Elizabeth S. VanDenBerghe, "Edwin Dharmaraju: Taking the Gospel Home to India,"
Ensign, April 1990, https://www.churchof
jesuschrist.org/study/ensign/1990/04
/edwin-dharmaraju-taking-the-gospel
-home-to-india?lang=eng.

5. VanDenBerghe, "Edwin Dharmaraju."

6. VanDenBerghe, "Edwin Dharmaraju."

7. "Facts and Statistics: India," Newsroom, The
Church of Jesus Christ of Latter-day Saints,
https://newsroom.churchofjesuschrist.org
/facts-and-statistics/country/india.

8. Rutherford, *Worldwide Church*, 72, 75.

Callout, p. 84: VanDenBerghe, "Edwin Dharmaraju."

Callout, p. 86: "Bengaluru India Temple,"
Temples of The Church of Jesus Christ of
Latter-day Saints, https://churchofjesus
christtemples.org/bengaluru-india-temple.

Callout, p. 87: VanDenBerghe, "Edwin Dharmaraju."

SHE BELIEVED: BEVERLY BROUGH CAMPBELL

1. "Interview of Beverly June Brough Campbell—Her Life Story Part 2—May 2003," audio recording, 15:34, FamilySearch, https://
www.familysearch.org/photos/artifacts
/62647484?p=12436857&returnLabel
=Beverly%20June%20Brough%20(KWZG

-PTW)&returnUrl=https%3A%2F%2Fwww
.familysearch.org%2Ftree%2Fperson%2Fme
mories%2FKWZG-PTW.

2. "Interview of Beverly June Brough Campbell."

3. "Interview of Beverly June Brough Campbell."

4. "Interview of Beverly June Brough Camp-
bell"; Susan Easton Black and Mary Jane
Woodger, *Women of Character: Profiles of
100 Prominent LDS Women* (American Fork,
UT: Covenant Communications, 2011), 59;
The Phil Donahue Show, "Mr. Phil Donahue,
Ms. Barbara Smith, Ms. Beverly Campbell,"
Multimedia Program Productions, aired
February 18, 1980, on WGN.

5. *Phil Donahue Show*, "Mr. Phil Donahue,
Ms. Barbara Smith, Ms. Beverly Campbell";
Black and Woodger, *Women of Character*,
58–59; "Interview of Beverly June Brough
Campbell."

6. Kenneth L. Alford, Lloyd D. Newell, and
Alexander L. Baugh, *Latter-day Saints in
Washington, DC: History, People, and Places*
(Provo, UT: BYU Religious Studies Center;
Salt Lake City: Deseret Book, 2021), 304–9,
313–14; Black and Woodger, *Women of
Character*, 59.

7. "Address Given by Elder M. Russell Ballard at Beverly June (Brough) Campbell's

Funeral," audio recording, FamilySearch
https://www.familysearch.org/tree/person
/memories/KWZG-PTW.

8. "Interview of Beverly June Brough Campbell."

9. Dennis B. Neuenschwander, "Reflections on
Establishing the Gospel in Eastern Eu-
rope," *Liahona*, October 1998, https://abn.
churchofjesuschrist.org/study/liahona
/1998/10/reflections-on-establishing-the
-gospel-in-eastern-europe?lang=eng;
Alford, Newell, and Baugh, *Latter-day Saints
in Washington*, 314–15.

10. "Beverly Brough Campbell," Deseret News
Obituaries, Legacy, https://www.legacy
.com/us/obituaries/deseretnews/name
/beverly-campbell-obituary?id=15571780.

11. "Address Given by Elder M. Russell Ballard."

Callout, p. 89: "Interview of Beverly June
Brough Campbell."

Callout, p. 90: "Interview of Beverly June
Brough Campbell"; "Special Olympics,"
Wikipedia, last modified May 15, 2022, 17:58,
https://en.wikipedia.org/wiki/Special
_Olympics; "Beverly Brough Campbell,"
Deseret News Obituaries.

Callout, p. 93: "Beverly Brough Campbell,"
Deseret News Obituaries.

SHE SANG: WYNETTA WILLIS MARTIN CLARK

1. Wynetta Willis Martin, *Black Mormon Tells
Her Story: "The Truth Sang Louder Than My
Position"* (Salt Lake City: Hawkes Publica-
tions, 1972), 18–19.

2. Martin, *Black Mormon*, 16.

3. Martin, *Black Mormon*, 29.

4. Martin, *Black Mormon*, 38–40.

5. Martin, *Black Mormon*, 49–55.

6. Martin, *Black Mormon*, 25.

7. Martin, *Black Mormon*, 59–61.

8. Martin, *Black Mormon*, 23.

9. Martin, *Black Mormon*, 63.

10. Martin, *Black Mormon*, 72.

11. Martin, *Black Mormon*, 73

Callout, p. 95: Susan Easton Black and Mary
Jane Woodger, *Women of Character:
Profiles of 100 Prominent LDS Women*
(American Fork, UT: Covenant Communica-
tions, 2011), 74.

Callout, p. 97: Martin, *Black Mormon*, 23.

Callout, p. 98: Black and Woodger, *Women of
Character*, 74.

SHE VOLUNTEERED: BECKY DOUGLAS

Becky, Douglas, interview by author Bekki Hood, Ephraim, UT, May 10, 2022.

1. Becky Douglas, "When God Brings Life out of Ashes," *Meridian Magazine*, last modified February 19, 2020, https://latterdaysaint mag.com/when-god-brings-life-out-of-ashes/.

2. "Our Mission: Learn about Our Three-Pronged Approach," Rising Star Outreach, https://risingstaroutreach.org/about-us/mission/.

SHE DEFENDED: EMELIA MOULD AHADJIE

Emelia Mould Ahadjie, interview by author Bekki Hood, Provo, UT, December 7, 2021.

1. Tad Walch, "How Ministering Helped Members in Ghana Overcome 'the Freeze,'" Church News, last modified May 30, 2018, https://www.churchofjesuschrist.org/church/news/how-ministering-helped-members-in-ghana-overcome-the-freeze?lang=eng.

2. Shalyn Back and Karlie Guymon, "Emelia Ahadjie: Leading in West Africa with Faith, Courage, and Enthusiasm," October 27, 2020, in *Latter-day Saint Women*, podcast, 38:03, https://podcasts.apple.com/fi/podcast/emelia-ahadjie-leading-in-west-africa-faith-courage/id1491361653?i=1000496368959.

SHE PERSISTED: SAHAR QUMSIYEH

Sahar Qumsiyeh, interview by author Bekki Hood, Ephraim, UT, May 10, 2022.

1. Sahar Qumsiyeh, "My Story," *Sahar Qumsiyeh's Blog*, http://saharqumsiyeh.blogspot.com/p/info-about-me_16.html.

2. Qumsiyeh, "My Story."
3. Qumsiyeh, "My Story."

SHE OVERCAME: MIHAELA GANEA KING

Mihaela Ganea King, interview by author Bekki Hood, Bountiful, UT, March 10, 2022.

1. Shalyn Back and Karlie Guymon, "Mihaela Ganea King – 'After the Trial of Your Faith,'" in *Latter-day Saint Women*, podcast, 49:39, https://www.churchofjesuschrist.org/media/collection/latter-day-saint-women-podcasts?lang=eng&track=/media/audio/lds-women-2021-03-0093-mihaela-ganea-king-after-the-trial-of-your-faith-a5647b7?lang=eng.

SHE SAVED: CECILIE LUNDGREEN

Cecilie Lundgreen, interview by author Bekki Hood, Bountiful, UT, February 8, 2022.

1. Cecilie Lundgreen, "The Lord Really Is Kind," interview by Eline Amundson, The LDS Women Project, http://ldswomenproject.com/interview/7815/.

SHE TRUSTED: MELISSA WEI-TSING INOUYE

Melissa Wei-Tsing Inouye, interview by author Bekki Hood, Layton, UT, January 17, 2022.

1. Melissa Wei-Tsing Inouye, *Crossings: A Bald Asian American Latter-day Saint Woman Scholar's Ventures through Life, Death, Cancer, and Motherhood* (Salt Lake City: Deseret Book, 2019), 2.

2. Inouye, *Crossings*, 183–85.

3. Inouye, *Crossings*, 211.

4. Inouye, *Crossings*, 113.

5. Inouye, *Crossings*, 201.

6. Inouye, *Crossings*, 196–97.

SHE EMPOWERED: YVONNE BARAKETSE NSABIMANA

Yvonne Baraketse Nsabimana, interview by author Bekki Hood, Layton, UT, April 29, 2022.

1. United Nations, "Rwanda: A Brief History of the Country," Outreach Programme on the 1994 Genocide against the Tutsi in Rwanda and the United Nations, https://www.un.org/en/preventgenocide/rwanda/historical-background.shtml.

2. United Nations, "Rwanda."

3. Yvonne Baraketse, "I Know that My Redeemer Lives," interview by Meredith Marshall Nelson, The LDS Women Project, http://ldswomenproject.com/interview/i-know-that-my-redeemer-lives/.

4. Nsabimana, "Résilience," https://nsabimana.com.

SHE LOVED: MELISSA TE'O LAURENSON

Melissa Te'o Laurenson, interview by author Bekki Hood, Bountiful, UT, December 18, 2021.

1. Melissa Te'o Laurenson, "You Will Be Blessed: The Story of Melissa Te'o," Pacific, The Church of Jesus Christ of Latter-day Saints, accessed January 16, 2022, https://pacific.churchofjesuschrist.org/melissa-te'o-you-will-be-blessed.

2. Laurenson, "You Will Be Blessed."

3. "God Said Yes!," Global Histories, The Church of Jesus Christ of Latter-day Saints, https://www.churchofjesuschrist.org/study/history/global-histories?lang=eng.

Acknowledgments

Thank you to my children for listening to my stories from the beginning. You inspire me every day.

Thank you to my parents for raising me in such a loving home. You made me feel like I could do anything.

Thank you to Rhonda Miller, Jessica Roberts, and Quinn Silcox for years of encouragement, honest feedback, and retreats full of yummy food and delightful conversations. You kept me going when the writing got hard.

Thank you to Juli Smith for giving my idea life with your beautiful designs. You gave me the courage to push "submit."

Thank you to Bekki Hood for your dedication, talented writing, and witty sense of humor. You made this project fun.

And finally, thank you to my sweet husband, Travis, for making me better since we were thirteen years old. Having someone who loves and believes in you is everything.   —EC

My deepest gratitude goes to my dear friend and coauthor, Emily Cushing. I feel so privileged that she reached out to me during her search for a coauthor, and I couldn't have asked for a better partner.

I am grateful for all of the people who read drafts of the vignettes and offered feedback and encouragement: my parents, Steve and Mary Hood; and my dearest friends, Tesia Tsai and Haley McInnis. I am also grateful to my siblings, work colleagues, and former professors who shared my excitement and passion about this book. —BH

Together, we are indebted to the BYU Faculty Publishing Service for their edits and the Harold B. Lee Library's Special Collections department for their assistance in locating records. Thank you to all those who helped us obtain photographs and copyright permissions. And thank you to the team at Deseret Book—Celia Barnes for her direction, Alison Palmer for her genius edits, the committees and beta readers for their feedback, and the BIPOC readers for their wisdom and sensitivity.

Above all, we are grateful for the inspiring women, as well as their descendants, who shared their stories with us. Without them, this book wouldn't have been possible. We are humbled by their authenticity, and we know their stories will empower girls and women everywhere.

Subject Index

This subject index is intended to help readers find specific topics that are addressed in the essays of this book. Readers can use this reference tool to focus their gospel study on a particular topic or to help prepare for a Church or home evening lesson.

ADVERSITY

Amanda Barnes Smith, 6–11

Aurelia Spencer Rogers, 18–23

Annie Gillies Parker, 30–35

Martha Ann Stevens Howell, 36–43

Helen Dowawisnima Sekaquaptewa, 56–63

Chieko Nishimura Okazaki, 76–81

Becky Douglas, 100–107

Mihaela Ganea King, 122–27

Cecilie Lundgreen, 128–33

Melissa Wei-Tsing Inouye, 134–39

Yvonne Baraketse Nsabimana, 140–45

Melissa Te'o Laurenson, 146–51

CONVERSION

Lilia Wahapaa Kaneihalau, 24–29

Auguste Kuhlmann Lippelt, 44–49

Helen Dowawisnima Sekaquaptewa, 56–63

Carmen Galvez O'Donnal, 70–75

Chieko Nishimura Okazaki, 76–81

Elsie Sreenivasam Dharmaraju, 82–87

Wynetta Willis Martin Clark, 94–99

Sahar Qumsiyeh, 114–21

Cecilie Lundgreen, 128–33

Yvonne Baraketse Nsabimana, 140–45

Melissa Te'o Laurenson, 146–51

COURAGE

Amanda Barnes Smith, 6–11

Aurelia Spencer Rogers, 18–23

Martha Ann Stevens Howell, 36–43

Irene Colvin Corbett, 50–55

Chieko Nishimura Okazaki, 76–81

Image Credits

Pp. 6, 12, 14, 17, 18: © By Intellectual Reserve, Inc.; pp. 11, 21, 30, 40, 47, 58, and 61 are in the public domain; p. 23: courtesy International Society Daughters of Utah Pioneers; pp. 24, 27: courtesy University Archives, Joseph F. Smith Library, Brigham Young University–Hawaii, HI 96762; p. 29: © Photohobbiest, shutterstock.com; p. 33: Jimmy Emerson, DVM/Flickr Creative Commons/CC BY-NC-ND 2.0; p. 34: courtesy L. Tom Perry Special Collections, Harold B. Lee Library, Brigham Young University, Provo, UT; pp. 36, 41: courtesy Utah State Historical Society; p. 38: courtesy University of Utah, Salt Lake City; pp. 43, 44, 46, 69, 79, 85, 86, 94: provided by the authors, p. 49: courtesy Geraldine Bangerter family; pp. 50–54: courtesy Don Corbett; p. 56: photograph by Robert R. Lewis; p. 62: courtesy Susanne Page, from her book *Hopi*; pp. 64–68: courtesy Grimm family; pp. 70–71: courtesy L. Tom Perry Special Collections, Harold B. Lee Library, Brigham Young University, Provo, UT; pp. 72–73, 75: courtesy O'Donnal family; p. 76: photograph by Don Busath; p. 82: courtesy Lata Moses; pp. 88, 91–92: courtesy Campbell family; p. 97: courtesy Zuma Press, Inc.; pp. 100, 103–4, 106: courtesy Becky Douglas; pp. 108, 111: courtesy Emelia Mould Ahadjie; pp. 114, 116–17, 119: courtesy Sahar Qumsiyeh; pp. 122, 126: courtesy Mihaela Ganea King, photos taken by Michelle Larralde Photography; pp. 128, 131–32: courtesy Cecilie Lundgreen; pp. 134–35, 137–38: courtesy Melissa Wei-Tsing Inouye; pp. 140, 144: courtesy BYU Photo; p. 142: courtesy Yvonne Baraketse Nsabimana; pp. 146, 149–51: courtesy Melissa Te'o Laurenson; p. 170: Emily Cushing, photograph by Sadie Cushing; Bekki Hood, photograph by Kristin Burgoyne.

About the Authors

EMILY CUSHING was raised in South Jordan, Utah, and met her husband in their middle school math class. Her love of learning led her to become a teacher. She earned a master's degree in teaching and learning at Brigham Young University and has taught, among other places, in Tonga, Myrtle Beach, and England. She currently teaches in the Education Department at Utah Valley University. She enjoys reading, running, traveling, living in foreign places, and, above all, spending time with her family.

BEKKI HOOD grew up in Collegeville, Pennsylvania, until she moved to Arizona for her education. Because of her love for writing, teaching, and helping others, she earned a master's degree in English at Brigham Young University and a master's degree in clinical mental health counseling at Idaho State University. She currently works as a counselor in Layton, Utah, and she teaches introductory writing courses at BYU. She loves visiting her family, spending time with friends, and crashing her parents' vacations.

We'd love to hear your story or the story of a remarkable woman you know. Please email us at shedidbook@gmail.com.